ARE WE DEAD YET?

BY
JOHNNY SAVAGE

TRAFFORD

• Canada • UK • Ireland • USA •

© Copyright 2006 Johnny Savage.
All rights reserved. No part of this publication may be reproduced, stored in a retrieval system, or transmitted, in any form or by any means, electronic, mechanical, photocopying, recording, or otherwise, without the written prior permission of the author.

Note for Librarians: A cataloguing record for this book is available from Library and Archives Canada at www.collectionscanada.ca/amicus/index-e.html
ISBN 1-4120-8925-5

Printed in Victoria, BC, Canada. Printed on paper with minimum 30% recycled fibre. Trafford's print shop runs on "green energy" from solar, wind and other environmentally-friendly power sources.

TRAFFORD
PUBLISHING™

Offices in Canada, USA, Ireland and UK

This book was published *on-demand* in cooperation with Trafford Publishing. On-demand publishing is a unique process and service of making a book available for retail sale to the public taking advantage of on-demand manufacturing and Internet marketing. On-demand publishing includes promotions, retail sales, manufacturing, order fulfilment, accounting and collecting royalties on behalf of the author.

Book sales for North America and international:
Trafford Publishing, 6E–2333 Government St.,
Victoria, BC v8t 4p4 CANADA
phone 250 383 6864 (toll-free 1 888 232 4444)
fax 250 383 6804; email to orders@trafford.com
Book sales in Europe:
Trafford Publishing (UK) Limited, 9 Park End Street, 2nd Floor
Oxford, UK ox1 1hh UNITED KINGDOM
phone 44 (0)1865 722 113 (local rate 0845 230 9601)
facsimile 44 (0)1865 722 868; info.uk@trafford.com
Order online at:
trafford.com/06-0681

10 9 8 7 6 5

DEDICATION

I dedicate this book to my precious wife Joanie, who encouraged and prodded me at times, to write this true story about my family.

Thank you God for sending me this beautiful Christian lady to comfort and encourage me during the twilight years of my life.

TABLE OF CONTENTS

ARE WE DEAD YET?	i
PREFACE	iii
SAVAGE CLAN REVIEW	1
JOHNNY WAS NO CHARLES ATLAS	4
UNNECESSARY POVERTY & IGNORANCE	7
MAMA GOES TO WORK	14
SYLVESTER TRIES TO STOP MAMA FROM WORKING	20
MAMA AND HER CHILDREN MOVE AWAY	24
AN ANGEL CAME CALLING	29
JOHNNY'S ABSOLUTE WORST ASS WHIPPING	33
FIELD TRIP TO HELL	37
BARE ASS IN CHATTANOOGA	40
SYLVESTER WAS SICK IN THE HEAD	44
SYLVESTER'S REVENGE	52
THE WRATH OF SYLVIA "MA-BARKER" SAVAGE	57
MOVING MAMA TO ATLANTA	72
HAROLD SAVAGE AND HIS RICH WITCH	75
HAROLD CAUSED A LOT OF ASS-WHIPPINGS	84
ROBERT *"Don't say it like that!"* SAVAGE	87
RAYMOND SAVAGE	112

JOHNNY SAVAGE	120
WINDFALL TO HEARTBREAK	132
RACISM and IGNORANCE	138
GOD SENT AN ANGEL TO TEST ME	146
BETTY SAVAGE	149
ON THE LIGHTER SIDE	153
BILLY "We must humor him" SAVAGE	158
BILLY THE NIGGER KILLER	171
BILLY "THE LANDSCAPE ARTIST"	174
BILLY'S "REPOSSESSION SERVICE"	179
BILLY'S BURNED BUTTER BEANS	182
SARAH'S HEMORRHAGE	185
A REAL MAN STOOD UP TO BILLY	187
SYLVESTER CAN'T LEAVE WELL ENOUGH ALONE	191
SCREAM OF DEATH	194
ROBERT NEVER SEES THE DOCTOR	196
ROBERT'S WEATHER ALMANAC 2005	199
DOLLAR-WEED INFESTATION CAN BE HAZARDOUS	201
MAMA KNOWS BASEBALL	204
MY BEST ALL TIME FRIEND	206
MAMA WAS OVERLY PROTECTIVE	211

EPILOGUE: THE SAVAGE CLAN

FATE OF BILLY AND SARAH'S CHILDREN	217
FATE OF BILLY AND SARAH SAVAGE	223
HAROLD'S OLD RICH WITCH VISITS MAMA	225
FATE OF BRUCE SAVAGE, SON OF JOHNNY	228
FATE OF SYLVIA, ROBERT AND JOHNNY SAVAGE	230
DOMESTIC VIOLENCE	233
FINAL CHAPTER	235
NOTES	237

ARE WE DEAD YET ?

A true story about one family's extreme suffering, grief and tragedy, that goes beyond the power of one's mind to comprehend.

A story so tragic, that for some, the only way out was suicide!

Only the names have been changed to preserve the memories of the victims and the dignity of those who survived.

PREFACE

I hesitated for many years, pondering if I should or shouldn't write this true story about my family. My greatest concern was for the living family members and other relatives directly related to my story.

I realize that some of the content could cause serious hurt and embarrassment to those family members who have survived, and who have suffered great tragic loss.

I also had to take into consideration the grief and embarrassment this story may cause the children of those who are now deceased.

Dead or alive, each played a central part in the lives of the Savage family and deserve some measure of dignity!

My major concern was for my mother; Sylvia Savage, who is now Ninety-six years of age. How would she feel about my writing this story and how would it affect her personally?

Out of respect for my mother, I had decided to keep my manuscript locked away until her death.

Later, I asked myself, would mama want me to publish this story at all?

I went to mama and revealed the text of my manuscript and

sought her permission to publish this book after her death. To my complete surprise, she made these comments:

"Everything that you've written is the truth!" "You only have one problem that I can foresee!" "You may not sell many copies, because nobody in their right mind will believe any of this!" "I wish you success with your book, but there's no need to wait till after my death to seek publication." "You have my blessing to go forward now, if you want!"

Nobody could comprehend how much it hurt me to relive the horrors of my past that I both witnessed and lived through.

To transpose into writing, the events I had buried deep in the back of my mind, was very difficult.

After writing all day, there were numerous times when I would awake from a cold sweat, thinking of the things that I'd written earlier in the day.

I must apologize to my Lord and to the readers for the obscenities printed in this book. I had to tell it just like it was, or not tell it at all!

The obscenities in this story represent the emotion, anger and hatred that I felt when I lived and witnessed the things printed here. Even then, they are mild in comparison to the horrifying incidents in our lives. May God have mercy on the Savage family, both living and dead!

Memoirs

There is little chronological order in the way I wrote or formatted this book. Over a period of almost three years, I wrote chapters as they came back to memory as flash-backs of my past.

Read and absorb each chapter as it's own little story. By the time you complete this book, everything will fall into place and any loose ends will be firmly tied together.

SAVAGE CLAN REVIEW

Sylvester Savage (Father of the clan)
An ignorant Tennessee Ridge Runner Hillbilly with an 8th grade education, who spent his whole life chasing skirts and womanizing anything classified as female. A man who was selfishly frugal, who caused much pain and suffering at the expense of his wife and the six-children, he never wanted in the first place.

A poor excuse for a father who was rarely referred to as daddy or father!

Sylvia Savage (Mother of the clan)
A God fearing woman destined to live in hell on earth! A gracious lady who never in her life, used alcohol or tobacco. A wife and mother, who rightfully so despised her husband, but loved, cherished, protected and cared for her children all the days of her life.

A woman who for survival, could stand her ground under extremely harsh conditions.

A woman who was so tough, that on occasion, was jokingly referred to by family members as; "Ma Barker!"

Billy Savage   (Oldest Son)
The meanest most sadistic son-of-a-bitch on the face of the earth.

Harold Savage   (Second Son)
A greed stricken loner who married an old rich witch for her money.

He abandoned his entire blood family and lived his life trying to prove he was better than everyone else. His old rich witch found him one morning dead in his bed. He died like he lived, lonesome, sick and grieving for his mother.

Betty Savage   (Only Daughter)
A self-centered, selfish loner, who distanced herself from her family for a life of poverty and hell, because she didn't think she was getting the sympathy she deserved. Dying of cancer, she had the opportunity to see her mother and several family members one last time the night before she died.

Raymond Savage (Twin Son)
A beautiful person who was loved by everyone. He lived every day expecting a call from some major corporation as a high salaried executive, but it never came. He lived his life with a champagne taste on a beer budget, until poor health stopped him in his tracks.

Depressed and frustrated, he literally ate himself to death.

Robert Savage   (Twin Son)
A die-hard bachelor, who had all the most beautiful women, but never found one he trusted enough to marry. He never accomplished anything what-so-ever in his life.

In his late-sixties, in poor health, drawing social security and piddling around at the flea-markets for five or six dollars a day, he still lives at home with mama!

Johnny Savage (Youngest son)
A hard working ambitious man, who spent his life at a mid executive level. The only family member who attended college.

A Pioneer, Grandmaster and National Champion in the martial arts.

A respected Christian gentleman who not only survived the hardships of the Savage family, but went on to overcome the heartaches of the past and found peace with God, his wife, children, grandchildren and great grandchildren.

JOHNNY WAS NO CHARLES ATLAS

I remember it was in 1947 when my teacher Mrs. Allsup was speaking to our 5th grade class at Annie Lytle Elementary School in Jacksonville, Florida.

The subject being taught is; "Health & Hygiene".

In a very highbred, intellectual and elegant tone of voice she said:

"I do not wish to embarrass anyone, but I want to demonstrate the effects of poor nutrition and the lack of needed dietary supplements during the early stages of human growth and development!"

"Johnny, will you and Jerry, please stand up?"

Jerry and I stood as Mrs. Allsup directed her statement to the class:

"Class, I want you to take a close look at Jerry's physique and physical structure". "Notice the weight, body structure and muscle tone in his arms and body."

"Now class, I want you to look at Johnny." "As you can see, he is under weight and compared to Jerry his health appears to be puny and malnourished."

"As you can see class, there is a good eight to ten pounds of muscle mass on Jerry that is not on Johnny and yet they are the same age."

"Now the reason for this is obvious." "I know for a fact, that Jerry drinks milk with every meal and he also takes a vitamin supplement every day."

"I also know that Johnny drinks coffee for breakfast and water or tea with other meals every day and has never, to the best of my knowledge, taken any type of daily vitamin supplement."

"Johnny has a skeletal structure, no body mass and little or no muscle tone."

"This class… is positive living proof, that without proper nutrition, milk and daily vitamin supplements your body will greatly suffer during the early stages of human growth and development."

Fifty-Three years later, as I look back on this incident in my life, I have never before or since, suffered a more embarrassing moment.

Standing before my classmates, I felt massive degradation and less personal worth than a filthy cockroach crawling across the floor.

This incident will remain burned into my mind till I die… even if God allows me to pass away of old age.

As for a balanced diet in our household, that was a joke. Mama did the best that she could with whatever Sylvester made available for her to cook.

Sylvester did all the grocery shopping that one could classify as far less than frugal. We usually had one pot of something a day as our meal. It could be soup, stew, noodles, beans, or sometimes spaghetti.

This is where the term, "pot-luck" was started! We called it "pot-lick" in our household because eight people eating out of one pot meant that the strong survived, or the weak reached the pot first.

Literally licking the empty pot wasn't a myth in our house!

Since I was the youngest and weakest of the clan, I always tried to make it home and to the pot first. This way, I was sure to get my fair share. If I didn't, and the others arrived before me, I then had a serious problem.

As for breakfast, there was never enough milk for cereal. We had cereal all right, but not things like Raisin-Bran, Corn Flakes, or Cheerios. Sylvester would only buy a cereal called "Puffed-Wheat!"

This was nothing more than small wheat particles filled with air. No sugar and lacking any resemblance of nourishment or flavor.

Puffed-Wheat only cost sixty-nine cents for a plastic bag the size of a standard pillowcase. The most tasteless crap that anyone could feed a child, but it was cheap and plentiful.

You couldn't eat Puffed-Wheat dry, so without milk it was just another target for the roaches!

As for my skinny, puny structure, it wasn't by choice. If the lack of milk or vitamins was the cause of my under developed body, then my father was to blame.

Because of his selfish frugal philosophy, only one-quart of milk a day was allowed in our house, to cover the needs of all eight family members.

As for vitamins, there was no way in hell that my father would waste his money on such things. I never knew there were things called vitamin supplements, until I was in my late teens.

Sometimes I wonder how I survived for as long as I have. Most of my siblings didn't make it to a ripe old age!

UNNECESSARY POVERTY & IGNORANCE

As I look back on my early childhood, it's now obvious to me that our family's poverty and ignorance was much greater than necessary.

We lived in poverty conditions that were self-inflicted by my father.

I can still see the small "Shotgun House" that we lived in for so many years. In the south, shotgun houses were the cheapest of living conditions and specifically built to accommodate poor families, who would migrate together in one section of town. All the houses were built the same, two family, two story wood frame houses lined up in straight rows, side by side, with only a few feet of walking distance between each house. If you farted real loud, your neighbor would shout obscenities across the alley at you.

Each house consisted of a front and back door that was perfectly in line, with a long hall between the two doors. Off the hall were three small bedrooms, a kitchen, a very small dining room and one small bathroom.

If you opened the front and back doors of the first ten houses and fired a shotgun through the center front door of the first house, the blast would travel through all ten houses, entering the front doors and exiting the back doors of each house, never striking anything in it's projectile path. That's why they were called shotgun houses!

These were constructed as low rent properties by scumbag landlords, who never responded to any complaints, regardless of how serious.

Once you rented a shotgun house, any problems that arose were the responsibility of the tenant and that was clearly understood.

Our living arrangements consisted of my father and mother who slept in the first bedroom, my twin brothers Raymond & Robert slept in the second bedroom with me, and my older brother Harold slept in the third bedroom. My sister Betty slept in a make shift bedroom, which was supposed to be a dining room, but was too small.

My oldest brother Billy was away in the Marine Corps, fighting the Japs.

Living conditions were pure hell at times. We had cockroaches so large, they actually flew like birds.

They had long wings and at night in total darkness, we could hear them flying all about our bedroom. The only way to escape them was to stay tightly tucked in with the covers over our heads. Even then, we could hear and feel them land on top of our covers, rest a while and then fly off again.

Lack of oxygen made our breathing difficult, but this still beat giving the roaches a target, by poking our heads out from under the covers.

My God, this still gives me shivers even today when I think about it!

My father would never waste his hard earned money on any exterminators. He would sleep with the roaches, just like the rest of us to avoid (in his way of thinking) spending his money foolishly.

I can remember mama buying a bug bomb now and then, when she could save fifty-cents, without my father knowing it.

She would set it off at night just as we went to bed. I guess we breathed more of the bomb spray than the roaches, but none of us died from it!

The roaches sure as hell would die! So many, that mama would have to sweep them out the back door in piles. This would slow them down for a few days, but they'd always come back just as strong as before.

Every time mama used the bug-bombs, we knew there would be one super cat-fight and cursing match between mama and the lady that lived upstairs on the second level. As you could expect, hundreds of roaches would run upward inside the walls from downstairs, trying to escape the poison fog that mama had unleashed.

When the family upstairs got up the next morning, there would be hundreds of dead roaches scattered about their kitchen floor, and a bucket full of mourning survivors looking on.

They knew immediately that mama had set off one of her bug-bomb foggers, which caused all hell to break loose. Roaches were a way of life for all of us, so we just learned to live with the filthy bastards!

Rats were just about as bad. We went to war every night with a herd of rats that lived with us.

Mama had received ten rat traps, free of charge, from the county health department, to help us in our war.

Every night, mama would set all ten traps about the kitchen and the area we used as a combination dining and living room. She would bait each trap with a small piece of cheese, and lock down the spring loaded steel "slammer", as we children called it!

Within hours of turning out the lights and going to bed, we could hear the slammer come down on a rat, like the snap of a whip.

We slept down the hall about thirty feet from the loaded traps, but we could still hear the agony of the dying rats, as they screamed; eeeeeeeeeeeh!, eeeeeeeeeeh!, eeeeeeeeeeeh!, eeeeeeeeeeh!

In the morning, mama would dump the dead rats in the garbage, and get the traps ready again for that night. I would see her strike a large wooden "kitchen-match" as we called them and run the flame over the steel-slammer and then over the wood surface of all the traps.

Mama said that no live rat would come near the traps where another rat had died, because they could pick up the scent of the dead rat that had previously occupied the trap. Running the open flame match with it's sulfur scent over the trap, would kill the smell of death and thus make the trap useable again!

We had no heat in our house what-so-ever. During the cold winter months, we thought we would freeze to death.

Some concerned neighbor friend of mama's gave us a small round kerosene stove that stood about three feet tall and was about twenty-four inches in diameter.

Our neighbors knew of our extreme living conditions, but they weren't much better off than we were.

My father considered heat as a non-necessity. He'd tell us that he grew up in Tennessee without heat in his house and it didn't kill him.

We never had hot water in our house, until I was in my teens. There was a hot water heater when my father rented the house, but he called a plumber and had the hot water tank removed from the property. No way in hell was he going to pay any big electric bills for heating water, that was unnecessary.

When I was born, I was brought into this house of hell and remained there until I was a teen, never knowing that houses actually had heat or hot water.

If we wanted any hot water to wash our faces or bathe, we would heat a pot of water on that old kerosene stove and then carry it down the hall to the bathroom sink or tub.

I'm so ashamed to admit this, but as God is my witness, I thought all the years that I lived in that house, that the second faucet (which we called a spigot) on the sink and tub was there for a spare. In other words, if one faucet ever went bad or broke, there was always a spare sitting there next to it for replacement!

I never dreamed that hot water was suppose to come out of it. Oh God, how ignorant I was then and how embarrassed I am today as I look back!

Christmas was never a surprise for us children. We knew when we got out of bed every Christmas morning, exactly what poor old Santa had brought us. It was always the same, a sock stuffed with some fruit, a kaleidoscope and a metal spinning top that must be pumped with a center handle.

The faster you pumped, the greater the spin and the louder it "whirred" some childish noise.

I think Sylvester got a good deal and bought a case of each. He then stored them someplace and gave us a fresh one every Christmas.

As I look back now, Santa must have been a full blown Alzheimer's patient!

Can't you just picture three teenage boys sitting on the floor, staring down a hole from the end of a kaleidoscope at pieces of colored glass, while spinning some stupid-ass top? ... We felt and looked like fools!

We were never allowed as children to have school friends stay over at night because of the conditions that we lived in. There was no room anyway and I thank God now that there wasn't!

Our family stayed sick with colds and flu all winter long. In those days, there was what we called a "Family Doctor." The family doctor would actually come to the house when an appointment was made. Some of the children would have to be near death before my father would allow mama to call the doctor and make a house-call.

I was only five years old, but I can remember one doctor visit to our house, when mama and I were both very sick with the flu.

Dr. Hayes gave me a shot and some cough syrup and then gave mama a shot. As young as I was, I can still remember the exact words he said to her; "Sylvia, it will be a damned miracle if you ever raise these children to be adults under these living conditions!"

Mama answered the doctor by saying: "I know this doctor, but under the circumstances, I'm doing the best that I can for my children!"

And God Bless her, she was!

Not one of Sylvester's six children was ever allowed to be examined by a dentist. No way in hell was Sylvester going to throw away his money on such trivial things as his children's teeth.

From our birth, until we were adults, not once did any one of us ever sit in a dentist chair.

I was seventeen years old, when I joined the U.S. Air Force.

At basic training, all military personnel are examined by a physician and a dentist. I remember so clearly, the dentist was examining my teeth when he said: " you don't have a filling in your mouth or any sign of a cavity!" "who was your dentist?"

I told him that he was the first dentist to ever look in my mouth. Naturally, he was curious and wanted to know how my teeth were so strong and clean without ever having made a visit to a dentist!

I remember the dentist laughing out loud when I told him the truth of the matter:

Mama did what she thought was best for all her children including the care of their teeth. She knew that my father would never pay for any dental care, so mama would scare the hell out of us to make sure that we brushed our teeth really hard three times a day!

Mama would tell us about once a month... that if we didn't brush our teeth real hard at least three times a day, she would have to take us to a doctor called a dentist.

She told all of us that a dentist was a special kind of doctor, who used leather straps to hold children down in a chair and then he would take a crochet-needle and scrape their teeth for about two hours... until they were clean!

Mama used a crochet-needle to knit doilies and other things

for the table or dressers. All the children knew what a crochet-needle was because we would sometimes watch mama knitting out on the front porch in her rocking-chair.

Mama would tell us that if we didn't want our teeth scrapped with a crochet-needle, then we must brush no less than twice every day.

Scared out of our wits, we chose to brush three times a day rather than meeting that sadistic doctor who got his thrills out of strapping screaming children into a chair and torturing them for hours!

Knowing that my father would continue his selfish frugal ways, with no concern for our health or the misery that we lived in, mama must somehow find a way to provide additional income to meet the basic living necessities for her children. Mama hoped to eventually find a way to leave Sylvester and provide a decent home for her children, free of torment, misery, stress, poverty and humiliation.

Mama must go find a job!

MAMA GOES TO WORK

Mama going to work every day for an eight-hour shift, brought about her greatest fear. That fear was having to leave her children alone!

This was a sacrifice of necessity if her children were to survive or have anything beyond total poverty.

I can remember the day she pulled all the children together while my father was at work. Mama sat us down and looked each one of us straight in the eyes and said: "if you don't remember anything else I've ever said to you, please know that what I'm saying now is for our survival."

"If you children are to ever have anything other than hand me downs, I must go to work." "You children will be alone all afternoon and evenings, because I could only find work from 3:00 P.M. until 11:00 P.M. as a telephone operator at Southern Bell Telephone."

"I'll leave your supper cooked and on the stove before I leave for work." "All you have to do is heat it up and eat."

"I'd appreciate it, if you children would wash the dishes before you go to bed."

"Your father is going to go crazy when he finds out that I took a job, because he wants me here for his selfish pleasures and to keep his shitty underwear washed."

"If any one of you gets yourself in trouble while your father and I are working, the Child & Family Services will make me quit my job and then we'll never have anything again."

"I'm begging you children to please watch out for each other, stay out of trouble, come into the house before dark and no fighting amongst yourselves."

"Do you understand how serious this is and what you must do to help me?"

We knew exactly what she was saying and we knew if we caused any problems, she would lose her job and even greater was the fact that my brothers and I would get a big-time ass whipping!

Mama never allowed Sylvester to whip us, so she accepted this responsibility with much enthusiasm. When we did something wrong and lied, she would on occasion beat the living shit out of all three of us to make sure she got the right one. I got many an ass whipping for something my brothers did and lied about and vice-versa!

We even got ass-whippings for things the neighbor's kids did, just because we were somewhere in the general area where the incident occurred.

If mama lost her job, it would cost all of us any hope of ever having anything that we could be proud of.

Just to have some decent clothes to wear to school would be a blessing! I could just picture myself owning a real pair of snug-fitting Levi jeans... that had never been worn by anyone else but me!

We called jeans "dungarees" in those days, just like we called sneakers "tennis-shoes"!

We all knew that mamas working would help to make our living conditions a little more bearable.

As I look back now at what mama said about living with hand me downs, nobody had to explain to me what she meant. We lived with hand me down clothes that people of this day in time wouldn't find fit to use as rags to polish their car.

Being the youngest, I received all my hand me downs when Raymond outgrew his clothes, then Robert got them, then I got them.

By the time I got the hand me downs, their value was about equal to that of shop-rags!

I can remember using safety pins to hold the shirtsleeve cuffs together or where a button was missing.

I always pinned my clothing from the inside, so my friends at school would be less likely to notice.

I remember when I didn't have enough safety pins, I'd use rubber bands to wrap around a button to make the button fatter, so it wouldn't easily pull free from the worn out button holes.

My hand me down slacks were far more critical than the shirts. Most of them had a good five to six inch overlap at the waistline, forcing me to pull the belt as tight as I could to keep my pants up.

There was so much extra material that it would bunch up in big lumpy pleats around my skinny waist. I'd punch holes in the hand me down belts with an ice pick to make them fit better.

I'd then tuck the six or eight inches of extra-unwanted belt inside my pants at the waist area.

All this extra work in getting dressed for school paid off as long as I could prevent my teachers or classmates from looking at my waist area. I hid this mess by never tucking my shirttails inside my slacks. With the shirttails out, all that horrible looking mess at my waist was concealed from the eyes of the world!

Hand me down shoes were part of my wardrobe as well. I must tell you about the shoes:

As children, we boys wanted tennis shoes. There was no such thing as "Sneakers" in those days. Only one athletic canvas shoe style that tennis players always wore. There was no arch in the old style tennis-shoes, just flat as a pancake, made of canvas, with shoe-strings twice as long as necessary.

Dear Lord how I would have loved to wear those tennis-shoes, but as with the other wardrobe, old Sylvester wasn't about to buy me tennis-shoes, when I had four older brothers to hand me down their shoes. I guess being the youngest wasn't so good where my wardrobe was concerned.

The hand me down shoes never fit me, regardless of which brother they came from. Usually they were too large and no matter how tight I pulled the laces the heels would slip up and down when I walked.

I always had a big runny-blister on my heels. Blisters were just something that I accepted and lived with. Thank God for Band-Aids, but even so, it's a wonder that I don't have cancers on both of my heels today.

I was so skinny, that I had an A-width foot. Most of my hand me down shoes were D&E widths, which allowed my feet to flatten out, resembling that of a duck's!

Because of this extreme abuse to my feet, I must wear prescription orthotics even today.

Then, there were the shoes with a big hole in the bottom center of the sole. I remember that I'd fold cardboard and place it in the center of my shoes, trying to keep my feet dry when it rained.

There were times when the soles would come loose on the bottoms of my shoes from the toe area to the heel. When I'd walk, the shoes would go; flap, flap, flap, flap!

I tried glue, but they'd only hold for a few hours before flap, flap, flap, again.

We didn't have "Super-Glue" in those days, just one glue called "Mucilage". It was OK for gluing paper, but not much else!

With everything that I wore in those days, I had to be creative and figure a way to make it look, fit or feel a little better. Regardless, I still looked like shit and a poor excuse for the human race.

When you have nothing to work with from the start… you can't expect to end up with anything that looks remotely presentable!

Having to go to school looking like this was so embarrassing and un-called for. My father was not a good provider when it came to our school clothes or school lunch needs.

Back in the 1940s, there was little or no welfare available like there is today. A sharp welfare recipient today can lie back on the couch watching soap operas on television while the Federal Government pays the rent, utilities, groceries, day-care and a little extra cash for pocket change!

Since my father worked for the railroad, we wouldn't have qualified for any welfare assistance anyway.

There was however, one minor welfare school lunch program available and old Sylvester damned sure took full advantage of that!

If under nourished children were singled out at school, the lunch program would provide a meal for twenty-five cents a day for an elementary grade child.

My father figured this one out in a hurry; "if I can get by with paying just twenty-five cents a day for the children's lunch... times three children still at elementary level, that would be seventy-five cents a day, instead of one-dollar and ninety-five cents."... "I will be saving one-dollar and twenty-cents a day, if I let the school feed them!"

"One-dollar and twenty-cents a day, times five days a week will put an extra six-dollars a week in my pocket... to spend on my women!"

In those days, that was a nice chunk of extra change for any workingman's pocket, so Sylvester jumped on this offer!

An average elementary school lunch menu for those qualifying for the twenty-five cent welfare program would consist of; a plate of hot stewed tomatoes poured over a single slice of white bread and one half-pint of milk. They would even throw in an extra cup of water to help wash it down!

Oh God, I still get nauseated even today, when I think back on that soggy, watered down tomato sauce soaked into a piece of white loaf bread. Try eating this when your classmates are sitting next to you with a plate full of hot spaghetti and meat sauce, a pint of milk, cake & ice cream. Sometimes I was so jealous and hungry just smelling their food that I wanted to cry!

If their fathers could send them to school with sufficient lunch money, then why did my father have to be so different, when it came to me?

My brothers and sister were no better off than I was. We all went through this torture, day after day and the same twenty-five cent welfare lunch!

I remember one occasion when I just couldn't get the stewed tomatoes down and just sat there looking at my lunch tray.

The teachers were so concerned about my need for nourishment that they made me sit at the teacher's table where they forced me to eat.

I pleaded with my classroom teacher not to make me eat the stewed tomatoes again, but out of concern for my health... she forced me, until I had to break from the table and run to the boy's rest room.

I remember so clearly that I got down on my knees over the toilet bowl and violently vomited, until tomato sauce spewed out of my nose. I can still feel the tomato acid as it burned my throat and nostrils!

For the longest time, I hated my teacher for making me eat that crap, but I was wrong. She wasn't trying to be mean or hurt me; she was doing whatever she had to do to get some nourishment into my skinny gut!

Although I realize this now, I still today... cannot stand the sight or smell of stewed tomatoes!

SYLVESTER TRIES TO STOP MAMA FROM WORKING

When Sylvester realized that his Sylvia had accepted employment, he absolutely blew his lid. Sylvester shouted in no uncertain terms that mama *could not* go to work and that he would stop her before she ever made her first day!

Mama told her beloved Sylvester that he'd better start now, because she was going to work the following day.

Since my father never allowed mama to drive a car or have a drivers license, he thought he could use this to stop her from going to work.

"Tell me Sylvia, just how in the hell do you expect to get to and from work?" "You don't have transportation or money for the city bus and I damned sure ain't gonna haul your ass to or from your job!"

"You listen to me you cheap bastard", mama shouted back! "I don't expect you to drive me to work and I wouldn't accept a ride from you, if you offered me one!"

Mama then shouted into my father's face; " I'll walk to and from work if I have to, but I'm damned sure going to be at work on time tomorrow... so you go to hell!"

That's exactly what mama had to do. She walked three miles to work every day arriving on time at 3:00 P.M. She then walked home three miles at night, after she got off work at 11:00 P.M.

I watched mama do this for a month before she got her first pay check. In those days, companies would always hold back two weeks pay, then another two weeks before you actually received any money.

During that month, I'd try to wait up for mama to come in from work because I was worried about her safety while walking in total darkness from downtown Jacksonville to our house.

I can remember times when mama would have to walk home in the pouring rain and cold. Sometimes she'd come home crying because some dirty old man tried to pick her up by offering her a ride.

Mama would be so scared and humiliated that she would be shaking.

I can only imagine that mama didn't have any money for lunch at the telephone company cafeteria during that first month and went without eating on her breaks. I do remember a few occasions when mama would start her walk to work, with nothing more than one banana in a small paper bag for her lunch.

Sylvester on occasion would stand on the front porch grinning like a Cheshire-cat, watching as mama walked off toward work. His precious Cadillac parked at the curb.

There were times, when Sylvester would actually get in his Cadillac, drive past mama who was walking to work, go park his car at the telephone company front entrance and wait for her to get there.

When mama arrived at the front entrance, Sylvester would be waiting and literally block the entrance with his arms outstretched across the walk-way.

Sylvester would stand there blocking her entry, until she was late for work. After mama was ten minutes or so late, he'd allow her to enter, watching her walk up the stairs crying!

Sylvester thought in his pea-sized brain, that if mama was late a few more times, she'd lose her job.

Regardless of the hardships, mama still held her ground, ignoring my father's threats and intimidation's until she drew her first pay check. From that day on, mama had the change she needed to ride the city bus to work.

Now for some people, this may not seem like such a big deal, that some woman had enough change to ride a city bus. To my brothers and I, this was a really big victory for mama. Just knowing that she no longer had to walk six miles a day, in all kinds of weather was a great relief for us and a victorious slap in the face to Sylvester!

As for mama being late for work a number of times, she had a very understanding shift supervisor, who not only listened to her reason for being late, but who also took strong action to stop Sylvester in his tracks.

Mama's supervisor notified Southern Bell's Security Department and had two uniformed security officers placed on surveillance at the front entrance door.

The next time Sylvester tried to block mama's entry to work, he was physically escorted off the property and warned that he would be arrested and jailed if he ever tried blocking the entrance again!

Sylvester was also issued a no-trespass warning, which barred him completely from the telephone company property!

Sylvester didn't accept defeat gracefully. He only changed his methods of attack. He started by writing nasty threatening letters to the executive officers of the telephone company.

He accused them of a cover-up by protecting a woman who had abandoned her children.

Sylvester wrote that Sylvia was not a fit mother, that she goes to work knowing that her four kids were unsupervised, without meals and alone until 1:00 A.M. Sylvester demanded that Sylvia's employment be terminated immediately!

With only an 8th grade education, Sylvester's letters didn't have much of an impact on the executive officers who read them. They then called mama into the corporate office for an interview.

Mama was allowed to read all the letters and the nasty accusations that Sylvester made against her.

Mama was embarrassed by both the content of Sylvester's letters and the poor grammar, spelling and punctuation in his writings.

Sylvester threatened to file a civil suit against Southern Bell Telephone Company for what he called a cover-up of child abuse and extreme neglect, if mama wasn't fired from her job!

Mama explained her situation in truth and detail to her employers. Expressing her extreme need to retain her job, mama assured the executive officers that she had neighbors who watched after the children until she arrived home. The children's meals were prepared every day before she left for work.

After realizing the extreme hardships that mama was living under, not only did the telephone executives totally support her, they also provided, at no charge to mama, a free taxi ride from the telephone company to the front door of our house *every night that mama worked!*

Thirty-five years later mama retired with a pension from Southern Bell Telephone Company, where she was then a member of management.

Mama still refused to ever accept a ride in Sylvester's precious Cadillac for all of those thirty-five years.

MAMA AND HER CHILDREN MOVE AWAY

There came a time when mama could take no more of Sylvester's shit!

Carefully calculating a budget on her meager telephone company wages, mama figured out that we could survive on our own without Sylvester.

It was 1949, when mama took Raymond, Robert, Betty and myself and moved to a small but new home way out in the middle of no-where. The new houses in that isolated area of Jacksonville sold for ten-thousand dollars, with one-thousand down and finance the balance. In that area, houses sold cheap because they were so isolated that few people were willing to live there, regardless of the sale price.

With mama's small salary, this was all she could barely afford, and when I say barely, I mean barely.

We never had a car, which helps me remember that there were no paved streets, just dirt and muddy roads for miles and miles. The closest bus stop was over a mile from our home.

Our home was small with three bedrooms and one bath. The most exciting things about our new home was for the first time in our lives, we had a hot-water heater and a large kerosene stove in the hallway that warmed the house on those cold nights. There was no air-conditioner, but that didn't matter, since we never had air-conditioning anyway!

Oh God, how wonderful it felt to take a hot bath and to snuggle under the covers on those cold nights, with that big kerosene-heater puffing out warm air and not have to worry any more about flying roaches.

Since mama worked for the telephone company, we also had a telephone, so mama was able to call us at night when she was working, to make sure we were all okay!

For the first time in our lives, we had hot bath water and a telephone. We were convinced that we were really coming up in the world.

Mama couldn't afford curtains at first because of the extreme difficulty in making the down payment on our home, so we hung old sheets and towels over the windows with tacks and nails.

Things were rough at times, because mama had to walk slightly over a mile to the bus stop so she could go to work. It wasn't so bad, since she used to walk three-miles to work when she first got her job at the telephone company.

I used to walk with mama to the bus-stop to keep her company and then walk home by myself after she caught her bus.

It was rough when it rained, because the wind and rain would soak both of us before we could walk the mile, even with an umbrella.

The worst part was the muddy roads. Mama would take an extra pair of shoes and nylon hose in a paper bag, so she could change into something dry when she arrived at work.

I used to feel so bad for mama when she'd get on the bus all wet, with mud caked on her shoes all the way up to her ankles.

I know that she felt just as bad when the bus pulled away and she'd see me out of the bus window, walking that mile back home in the pouring rain. We did what we had to do!

Although mama was on her own to get to work every day, I thank God again, because the telephone company still provided mama a taxi-cab ride home right to the front-door after she got off work at 11:00 P.M.

We children had a really tough time getting to and from school as well. We walked most of the time, rain or shine.

Sylvester wasn't allowed to move with us and remained in that old shotgun house on Edison Avenue. He was mad as hell, because he absolutely must have someone to cook for him, wash his clothes and clean his house. With mama gone, he was totally helpless!

Sylvester would call mama about once a day, threatening and cursing her with demands that she move back to Edison Avenue.

Looking back on this episode in my life, I can remember as if it was yesterday, the greatest hardship and misery that we suffered, was for the lack of food.

Sylvester refused to provide any support what-so-ever to help mama with the expenses or utilities at our new home.

To keep from ending up in court, he did agree to buy Raymond, me and Robert one new pair of dungarees, once a year for Easter and to provide mama with twenty-five dollars every two weeks for food. There was absolutely no way that mama could stretch this out for two weeks and feed her children anything considered reasonable.

Sylvester's plan from the start was to use food or the lack of it to starve us out and he eventually succeeded!

Every day, our meals were an adventure. We ate tons of beans, soup and vegetable stew for the fourteen months that we lived in our new home. Meat was a rarity and a big treat when we did have any.

Mama asked the butcher at the super market to save hambones or beef-bones that were usually thrown out and she would pick them up.

Mama would use the bones to help flavor the beans, soup or stew. I know he wasn't suppose to, but that butcher would on occasion leave a little extra meat on some of the bones. This was to help her in preparing something with a little more flavor for her children. I guess he felt sorry for us and I'm glad he did!

Our favorite, meal which wasn't often, was mama's old fashion southern "chicken & dumplings."

Only on occasion could mama afford to buy a baking-hen at the super market, which she would boil in a pot of water until the chicken fell off the bones. She would then add the dumplings which were made from rolling flour and water together and slicing into strips. After the dumplings simmered in the chicken-broth for about thirty-minutes, you had some really good eatin! We would get the good stuff like chicken & dumplings on Sundays, when mama was home with us for the week-end.

At school, we were still on the underprivileged children's lunch program, that I called the welfare lunch. The meals at Jr. High School were a little better than that of the elementary level, but it was still a welfare lunch just the same.

We usually had something like "beenie-weenies", a roll and a half-pint of milk, which I liked. Sometimes we had something that looked like hash and on occasion spaghetti.

I had adjusted to the welfare-lunch menu since elementary school, so I knew that I could handle it okay. The one thing that I hated most was the fact that all the welfare-lunch children were given a plastic sign to sit on their trays, which indicated that we were the recipients, or poor white trash of the welfare menu. This little plastic sign sitting on my tray let the servers behind the lunch line know that they were not to give us any of the good stuff!

Walking through that lunch line with my school mates and my little plastic sign was so embarrassing. Although the sign was only three by three inches, to me it was like having a neon sign across my back that was flashing the words; "hey everybody, look at little Johnny with his skimpy beenie-weenies!" God, I was so embarrassed.

Mama fought off the hunger wolf at our door for over a year. Sylvester still refusing to give mama one dime more to help feed us.

We didn't have one ounce of animosity toward mama, when she had to rent out our new home, swallow her pride and move us back to the old shotgun house on Edison Avenue with Sylvester and his roaches.

Mama grieved for years over having to make that decision to subject her children to Sylvester's shit again, but she had to do what she had to do!

None of the children wanted to move back to that old Edison Avenue house, after having experienced the luxury of hot water and heat in our new home.

We even tried to bargain with mama that we'd eat less to save money if we could stay in our new home, never realizing how ridiculous our suggestion was.

In the end, we all moved back to Edison Avenue with Sylvester and the cock-roaches, to once again experience the miseries of hell on earth.

As for my precious mama, I realized in later years, that she did what she did to keep her children from suffering the results of malnutrition. Our health was more important to mama than her pride!

Mama rented out the new house to a Navy Officer for enough to cover the mortgage payments.

After three years, the "shot-gun" houses on Edison Avenue were condemned and we were able to move back to mama's new house.

Sylvester was allowed to come live with us this time, but it was always mama's house. God Bless You Mama.

AN ANGEL CAME CALLING

I was six years old when an earth-shattering traumatic experience brought me close to a heart attack. My heart pounded so hard that I could feel it banging against my undershirt. Fear gripped me so tight in the chest, that I fainted!

I am 68 years of age at this writing and I can still remember the incident as though it happened last night.

God sent a Guardian-Angel to confront me. I'll never know why, until I get to Heaven, look my Saviour in the eyes and ask Him.

Anyone with any common sense would immediately conclude; "if this was an Angel sent by God to confront a child, then all fears would have been erased before hand!" "God wouldn't scare a child half to death with one of his Angels!"

I don't have the answer, but I am convinced that God had his reason. It could have been to strengthen the muscles in my heart, or to elevate the blood-flow through my body, who knows?

What I do know is that nothing since in my life has ever come close to the fright that I experienced back then.

It all started one night about 2:00 A.M. I slept in a crowed bedroom with my two eight year old twin brothers, Raymond and Robert.

Robert and I slept in a double bed, while Raymond slept in a single.

We were all fast asleep, when without cause or reason, my eyes suddenly popped wide open. I laid there wide awake for about a minute just staring up at the dark ceiling.

My attention and curiosity was suddenly motivated when a glow or light at the foot of my bed caught my eye. Fear of the unknown gripped me, but I just couldn't leave well enough alone. I had to look!

Standing there just inches from my feet, was a beautiful female-Angel, in all of her glowing, glorious aura. She wasn't just looking at me, she was staring me in the eyes with what felt like fire!

Her expression was one of warmth, love and peace. She was smiling and appeared to be wearing a soft, silky bright-white gown that was glowing like a light. Her arms were at her side and she was of average height and weight.

There was no doubt in my mind, even at six years of age, that I was looking at a real live Angel. I was so gripped with fear, that I was unable to shake or wake Robert or Raymond. I just laid there frozen in my track, closed my eyes and fainted from the pounding in my chest!

I awoke with the others that morning and told everybody in my family what had happened to me. Some laughed at me while the others just teased me about having a nightmare. I knew better!

Who in their right mind would believe such a story from a six year old boy?

I tried to stay busy and occupy my memory from my fears of the night before, but it still haunted me all day.

At bedtime, I fought going back into that room, but had no choice in the matter. My mama tried to assure me that it was a dream and that it wouldn't happen again.

I fell asleep shortly after crawling into bed with Robert and slept sound until (you guessed it) 2:00 A.M. Bam!... my eyes popped wide-open and there she was. Same place, same time, just smiling and staring me in the eyes. I fainted again, just short of a full blown heart-attack! Nobody believed my story, even though it happened night after night for the next five days.

To calm me down, mama tucked me into bed that night and made sure there were no clothes or blankets hanging on a doorhook or draped over a dresser that might look like a person standing in the dark.

By this time, my brother Robert who had OCD, was starting to get even more nervous than his usual self. He was starting to believe that there had to be some truth in my story, but wanted no part of it.

After falling asleep, I was awakened by Robert later in the night. He whispered to me; "I gotta go pee and I'm afraid to go by myself!"

The bathroom was down the hall a ways from our bedroom and he wanted me to go with him.

Everything seemed calm at the time, so we crawled out of the bed and started to walk. Just as we reached the foot of the bed, I spotted the Angel standing slightly to the wall side of the foot of the bed. She was staring at me and less than three feet from us.

I had to prove to Robert that I was telling the truth about the Angel.

As scared as I was, I still had the energy to stop in my tracks, grasp Robert's right arm and turn him to face my Angel.

When Robert saw her, he turned so white from fear, that he almost glowed too! Without a word, he turned and wobbled straight back to bed, with me close on his heels. We crawled under the covers, never spoke a word and shook like a leaf until we both passed out.

The next morning, I told mama what happened and received some of the same humorous comments as in the past. Mama was concerned, but helpless to do anything about what was happening.

That day, mama got with my sister Betty who was thirteen years old and made up a good story in an effort to calm both me and Robert.

Betty came to me and told me that what I was seeing at night was her, that she would come to our bedroom some nights to check on us and to make sure we had enough blankets on our beds.

Betty apologized for scaring us and told me not to worry anymore.

She said that she wouldn't visit our bedroom again at night.

By this time, I was so scared and emotional, that I took her story literally and welcomed any explanation for what was happening.

That night, calmer and sound asleep, my eyes popped-open again at 2:00 A.M. I had to look and there she was. In all her brightness and glory, there stood my sister Betty,... so I thought!

Being completely convinced and trusting my sister, I got out from under the covers and crawled to the foot of the bed calling out her name; "Betty, "Betty."

I stood straight up on my knees, placing my face directly in front of the face of the lady standing there.

Just inches away, I stared directly into her eyes, as I continued to say two or three times; "Betty, is that you?"

I immediately knew why Betty didn't answer me, because I could clearly see that this wasn't Betty.

I was nose-to-nose with a beautiful woman in her late 20s or early 30s!

This was without a doubt, an Angel on a mission from God!

Only God knows how I was able to turn around and crawl back to my pillow and under the cover. At that point, I just knew I was a goner. I was so gripped with fear, that I didn't care if I did die!

I know that I'll never know the meaning of this Angelic visit, until I am on my death bed or until I get to Heaven and ask God himself.

The Angel never returned again and until this day, Robert is still too frightened to talk about it!

JOHNNY'S ABSOLUTE WORST ASS WHIPPING

Mama was bad about volunteering my brothers and I for boring freebie duties for whatever the neighbors or her friends needed.

She would loan us out to help neighbors in moving their personal belongings, loading pick-up trucks or rental trailers. Mama would tell the relocating neighbors that it wasn't necessary to pay us, that the children were more than happy to help them in their relocating.

This was bullshit to me and my brothers, who had worked our asses off all day. We wanted at least some pocket change for our physical labors! Nevertheless, we'd come home as broke as when we left.

I couldn't have been more than seven or eight, when mama volunteered my services to baby-sit a young neighbor child, while it's mother did her grocery shopping. It was a no-brainer job, requiring that I just sit and watch the little tot for a couple of hours.

If I had a problem, my mama was just a holler-away, right next door.

Our next-door neighbor lived upstairs on the second floor of a two-story "shot-gun" house just like ours.

I was quite pissed off at mama for volunteering me to babysit, without any prospect of financial compensation, but I had no choice in the matter.

I remember that the mother had left me and the baby to play, while she shopped. I was plenty bored and mad, when I discovered the back porch of this upstairs rental was stacked to the ceiling with old newspapers.

In those days, people would collect old newspapers (called a paper-drive) and sell them to a government pick up service for recycling. This was during the time of war and many items were recycled for small change.

I think the old newspapers would bring about a penny for every ten-pounds collected.

I had never seen so much newspaper stacked in one place and it excited me.

I found some big wooden kitchen matches, so I took the baby with me out on the back porch and decided to start me a small bon-fire. Nothing big was intended, just a small fire to entertain us.

I fluffed me a small pile of newspaper on the porch floor and struck a match to it. The baby and I sat there and enjoyed the bonfire for a minute or so, when I suddenly noticed that a much larger stack of newspaper was also burning.

I desperately tried to put the fires out, but the harder I stomped the burning paper, the more the sparks and flames flew!

Before I knew it, the whole back porch was in flames. I didn't know what to do, other than to take the baby in my arms, walk down the back porch stairs and over to my house.

I was too afraid to go in and tell mama, so I crawled under my house with the baby and hid. All hell broke loose about five minutes later.

I could hear mama screaming and crying. I could hear fire engine sirens blaring with people, police and firemen running up and down the alleys separating the houses.

I could hear screams of: "where are the children?", "Where's the baby?" It was horribly frightening, so me and the baby sat very still and very quiet.

This pandemonium went on for about two hours, until the firemen had raked and cleared the burned newspapers off that back porch, looking for two small charred bodies.

When they concluded that no charred bodies were there, they started a detailed inch-by-inch search of the neighborhood.

You guessed it, in about fifteen minutes; a police officer shined his flashlight into our faces where we were hiding under mama's house.

They pulled us out from under the house, where more pandemonium broke out.

Some people were crying, some were cheering and everybody was hugging and kissing me and the baby. I thought I was some kind of hero, until all the excitement ended, the police and firetruck had gone and mama got me back inside our house.

Mama explained to me that she had to punish me for setting the neighbor's back porch on fire. That this was going to hurt her more than it would hurt me. That again, was bullshit!

Mama couldn't just whip me, she had to make an example of me and did such a good job, that all the neighbors on the block where we lived, knew that I was being punished for what I did.

This meant, that the physical blows and my screams would have to be plenty loud to cover a one-block area, so everybody could hear.

With all the windows in the house open, mama started to flail the hell out of me, with everything that she could find as a weapon.

This beating went on forever and I thought she would never stop.

Mama beat me so long and so hard, that when she was finished, she started to cry. Mama knew that she went too far in punishing me and got so caught up in her frenzy, that she couldn't control her actions or stop the beating within reason.

I thank God, that He spared both me and the baby. I'll never forget that incident as long as I live. I am sixty-six now and my ass still hurts from that whipping!

Until this day, mama remembers and regrets giving me such a fierce beating and boy so do I!

Needless to say, I never played with matches again.

FIELD TRIP TO HELL

I was ten years old, in the fourth-grade at the Annie Lytle Elementary School in Jacksonville, Florida. It was time for our annual field trip and the class had voted to spend a long day at Kingsley-Lake, a popular swimming, picnic and recreation site.

It didn't matter to me where the class went, because I always had a good excuse ready, as to why I wouldn't be going. I always made the excuse that I was sick or there was an emergency in my family or that my grandma died.

My grandma must have died at least ten times during grammar school alone!

It wasn't that I didn't want to go to the lake like the other kids, it was that I was just too embarrassed to go. My father was never too eager to get off his wallet so I could pay my trip dues or have any money to eat on during the day.

A person never gets more hungry in their life, than when spending a full day swimming, running and playing. There is just something about swimming for hours that brings out a mammoth appetite, that must be fed.

While the other kids were stuffing themselves with hot-dogs, hamburgers, potato-chips and soft-drinks, my brothers and I would have to go off and hide, so as to not bring unwanted attention from the other classmates!

If we were asked why we weren't eating, we would always say that we weren't hungry and that mama was having a big meal ready for us when we got home. All the while, we felt like our stomachs were eating our back-bone and using our ribs for toothpicks!

Another reason why I wouldn't go on the field-trips was because I was ashamed of my undernourished, skinny, puny body with my ribs sticking out. I never owned a decent pair of swimming trunks, other than old hand me downs that were three sizes too large. There was always enough slack in the seat of my trunks to make an elephant an underskirt.

Well anyway, the big field-trip day arrived, so I stayed home with no intention of going. This time, my lying excuses caught up with me, because my teacher knew that I didn't have the money to pay my dues or to eat, so she got with some other teachers and took up a collection to pay my way.

If that wasn't embarrassing enough, she made it worse, by talking the school bus driver into driving the entire class over to my shabby residence to pick me up.

Our house was in such poor condition, that it wouldn't have even qualified for urban-renewal status and here my whole damn class is staring at the slums, in shock!

I was in greater shock, that all my classmates are sitting there on the bus, parked in front of my shack. They were peering out the bus windows as if watching a Panoramic movie, all the while waiting for me to surface.

I'm hiding in the front room, carefully peeking out the window as not to be seen by my classmates.

My teacher is at the front door asking mama if she'll allow me to go on the field-trip, while mama, knowing that I don't want to go is trying to make excuses.

This embarrassing situation was nothing short of hell on earth. I was too embarrassed to even consider making that trip. I knew that all my classmates were now aware that I was too poor to make the trip and lived in sub-standard housing, that most of my classmates had never seen up close before.

I know that the conversation between mama and my teacher only lasted a few minutes, but it seemed like hours before the school bus finally drove away with me still peeking out the window to make sure they were gone.

Returning to school was really tough, because I knew there would be a lot of embarrassing question for me to answer and I would again be forced to come up with more lies!

BARE ASS IN CHATTANOOGA

Poverty breeds ignorance and the reverse also applies. Being raised in both, my brothers and I were trapped to it's fate!

Sylvester was our father, but never fulfilled the role as a daddy. He greedily hoarded his income at the expense of his children, denying us even the bare essentials at times.

Sylvester worked for the Atlantic Coast Line Railroad all of his adult life.

In those days there was always a long waiting list of men wanting railroad jobs. Railroad men were considered to have greater than average incomes.

About fifteen years into his job, the railroad officials offered him a supervisor position as Yardmaster, which Sylvester jumped at the opportunity to accept.

Once promoted, my older brother Harold, figured out that my father was only making minimum wage of $1.35 per hour, because they required him to work twelve-hours a day, seven-days a week, with no overtime pay included. He actually took a severe cut in pay as an hourly employee when he accepted this salaried position.

Explaining this to old Sylvester was a waste of time, because as he said; "it's worth something to be boss!"

There was one good perk in my father's new position, where he received an annual pass for him and his family to ride the passenger trains.

Shortly after receiving his new position, Sylvester decided to take his annual vacation and go visit relatives in Oneida, Tennessee.

Mama knew that Sylvester would whore-around, if he was allowed to vacation alone, so she insisted that Sylvester take Raymond, Robert and myself along with him. There was no way in hell that mama would ever take a trip with him and he knew it!

Traveling with three children didn't settle too well with him, but he knew there was no need to argue with mama about it!

Mama packed our raggedy clothes in a suitcase and fussed with Sylvester because none of us had a decent pair of underwear.

Mama insisted on two things before Sylvester got on the passenger train with us; that he would schedule time for us to rest and that he would stop and buy us some new underwear at the first department store we saw.

I remember that I was seven and both Raymond and Robert were nine. We enjoyed the train ride and nobody but us, knew that we were bare-ass under our dungarees.

The passenger train had a layover in Chattanooga, Tennessee until morning, so Sylvester decided to look for a place for us to sleep.

It was early enough yet to find a store and buy us some underwear, but Sylvester decided to look in the phone-book for an old friend that he grew up with. He found his friend's telephone number and called him.

My brothers and I were hovered next to the telephone booth for over an hour, shivering in the cold, like a dog trying to shit peach-pits. Sylvester and his old buddy "Vernon", just kept on talking and reminiscing.

As the evening got darker and colder, we overheard Sylvester make the comment; "I don't want to put you out Vernon, that might be too much on your family!" Sylvester then said; "are you sure, you have enough room for the four of us?"

Now it didn't take a rocket-scientist to know that old Vernon was trying to get Sylvester to bring us children and spend the night at his house. My brothers and I immediately chimed in, telling Sylvester that there was no way we were taking our bare-asses to spend the night in some stranger's house.

Old Vernon must have asked Sylvester what was wrong, because he put his cheap-ass blame on us, by commenting; "when my children packed for this trip, they were so excited they forgot to pack their underwear!"

He should have told old Vernon that he was too cheap to buy us decent clothing and that we didn't own any underwear, other than hand-me-downs that weren't fit for polishing rags!

Old Vernon came up with a solution; "tell the boys, that they don't need to be embarrassed, they can sleep in the bedroom with my two teenage sons!"

Like this was satisfactory to me and my brothers? Hell no, we weren't about to go into a stranger's house and sleep with his two teenage sons in our bare-ass condition. I could just picture two strange teenagers, in their toasty warm, flannel pajamas, welcoming three strange young bare-ass boys into their beds. Bull-shit, it just wasn't going to happen and we raised so much hell, that Sylvester finally told old Vernon that he'd see him on his next trip.

Now, Sylvester was mad, because he had missed free lodging and a couple of free meals. He looked in the telephone book for a Y.M.C.A., where we finally ended up spending the night.

I remember that Sylvester paid $1.50 for our room and he refused an additional room for $1.00 more.

In taking only the one room, there was just one double bed and two chairs. Sylvester promptly slipped off his slacks and got in the bed.

He slept in his underwear, knowing that his three boys were still bare-ass naked under our dungarees.

My brothers and I were still too embarrassed to sleep naked, so we slept in our clothes. I laid across the bed where Sylvester was sleeping and Raymond and Robert slept sitting up in the two available chairs.

We never did get any underwear until we arrived by train in Oneida, Tennessee the next evening.

I learned one thing through all of this, never travel anywhere in your bare-ass.

In the future, I would just keep my skinny-ass at home!

SYLVESTER WAS SICK IN THE HEAD

Sylvester had some strange perverted ways. He would aggravate the hell out of mama on his days off. He would read the obituaries in the morning paper searching out names of men near his age who had died in the past few days.

Sylvester didn't know the deceased, but he thought the poor widow left behind would need a man to service her sexual needs in time.

He would get all dressed-up in his best suit and tie, then go to the funeral hoping for a chance to look over the widow and make a new contact!

Sylvester thought in his ignorant uneducated mind, that the widow was now at her weakest point and that he could actually offer comfort that would eventually lead to a relationship.

He would introduce himself to the widow as a friend of her deceased husband, when in fact, he didn't have the slightest idea or care who that poor bastard was lying in the casket.

If things looked promising, old Sylvester would make contact with the widow a few weeks after the funeral, offering to take her to dinner.

Sylvester would make a pass at anything wearing a skirt. None of mama's friends would come around the house if Sylvester was home, because he had hit on all of them at one time or another. Sylvester thought the direct approach was always better in dealing with women.

In other words, catch one alone, run your hand up her skirt and grope her before she knows what happened!

If she screamed, which they all did, Sylvester would give out a big horse-laugh and try to make it look like some innocent playful prank!

Mama stayed embarrassed all the time and was always apologizing to her friends for Sylvester's ignorant perverted shit!

I remember one day when Robert stopped by my parents house with his girlfriend, who was a real beauty. Her name was Laura and she looked like she just crawled out of a "Penthouse Magazine".

Robert was twenty-one at the time and worked for the Seaboard Coastline Railroad.

While at our parents house, Robert got a telephone call from the railroad requesting that he report for work immediately due to some emergency. Sylvester offered to give Laura a ride home.

As Sylvester was driving Laura home, without any warning, he thrust his hand up her dress and grabbed her directly between her legs. Laura screamed for Sylvester to stop the car and let her out.

With his horse-laugh, Sylvester told her to stop screaming and he would take her home, that he was only playing with her!

Laura told Sylvester that if he didn't stop the car now, she'd open the door and jump out.

Sylvester didn't stop and she did jump, at forty-five miles per hour.

Laura ended up in the hospital all battered and bruised. She stayed for about a week.

As usual, Sylvester got out of this mess without a scratch, reporting to the police that the car door flew open accidentally and that Laura fell out. (Cars in those days didn't have seat belts).

For fear of costing Sylvester his job with the railroad, the whole thing was covered up. This did however, cause an even greater division between Robert and Sylvester, as if there could be a greater division than was already there!

There were so many incidents involving Sylvester and his extra marital affairs, that it would take a book as large as the "World Book Of Knowledge" to print them all. I will briefly mention three others that come to mind and then I will close out this chapter with a shameful incest that I wish I could forget.

I remember once when mama caught Sylvester at a widow's house in St. Augustine, Florida. Mama called the widow's son and had him meet her in St. Augustine.

They drove to the widow's house and the son went inside and caught Sylvester doing his thing with the widow.

All hell broke out when Sylvester came running out of the house half-dressed with the widow's son right on his ass.

Mama couldn't help but laugh as she watched that man chasing old Sylvester down the street and out of sight.

The widow's son didn't catch Sylvester and came back to the house verbally attacking his mother for her sinful ways.

I know that Sylvester thanked God that he was able to out run that widow's son!

I remember once when mama caught up with another of Sylvester's whores in a shopping area. She chased her past the stores, until the woman ran through the front door of a "Leggett's Drug Store" and right out the back door where she escaped. The good Lord was either watching over that woman, or mama.

Mama would have put a hurtin on that woman if she had caught her!

Another time, mama invited a man and his wife over to the house for a visit. The couple were former friends of mama and Sylvester and thought they were going to have a nice visit with cake and coffee.

Instead, while all four were sitting in the living room, mama told the husband that while he was working, his wife was sleeping with Sylvester and then mama somehow proved it!

I was sitting on the front porch, when that man blew-up and chased Sylvester out the front door of our house. I didn't know what was going on, but I too got tickled when I saw old Sylvester running around the corner up Riverside Avenue with that man right on his ass. I don't remember if he caught Sylvester or not, but I do know that Sylvester thought better of ever visiting that man's wife again!

Sylvester was sick in the head to the point that he even took advantage of his only daughter. I remember when my sister Betty was a really cute teenager and wanted to go to the school prom.

She didn't have any money to buy a new dress and was very depressed and sad.

Betty was standing at the kitchen sink washing dishes one afternoon, while mama was at work. I was standing on the back porch directly outside the kitchen door, when Sylvester walked into the kitchen and asked Betty; "why the sad face, have you been crying?"

Betty explained her problem to Sylvester and told him how badly she wanted to go to the prom, but was embarrassed to wear any of her old dresses.

Sylvester asked Betty how much money she needed for a new prom dress and she told him what she had found while shopping around.

I never will forget, Sylvester pulled his wallet out of his back pocket and handed Betty enough cash to purchase her new prom dress.

I was about as shocked as Betty, when Sylvester did this, but it didn't take long to find out why he was being so generous.

Sylvester didn't see me on the back porch, but I could clearly see him when he walked up behind Betty, reached around her waist with his arms, pulled her to him as he ground his penis into the butt area of Betty's dress. He also groped her breasts and her vaginal area with his fat sweaty hands.

When Sylvester had his fill of feels, he walked out of the kitchen. Betty was so humiliated that she stood there crying like a baby, as I sadly watched. I had never before seen anything like that and being as young as I was, I couldn't fully grasp what I had just witnessed.

To the best of my knowledge, Betty never told anybody what Sylvester did and neither did I. This was the price that Betty had to pay to get her new prom dress.

About five years later, another incident happened in our kitchen area, where Sylvester had said or did something to Betty, that caused her to come unwound.

Betty started screaming at Sylvester and grabbed a butcher knife from the counter and tried her best to kill him.

Mama walked into the kitchen about that time and to prevent Betty from killing Sylvester, she grabbed the blade of the knife as Betty was swinging.

Mama caught the blade in her hand causing a severe laceration between her thumb and fore- finger. I remember that it took a trip to the hospital and many stitches to close that awful gash!

One thing for sure, Betty had every intention of burying that butcher knife into Sylvester's chest and would have done so if mama hadn't intervened.

I'm both amused and amazed as I think back on Sylvester's ignorance and the things he did.

There was another incident when Sylvester got all dressed-up in his best suit and tie, telling mama that he had an appointment with a judge at the court-house, to officially and legally have his name changed.

Mama didn't offer any objection, because she never did like the "hill-billy" name of Sylvester in the first place.

When Sylvester returned from the court-house, he was all smiles and proud to announce his new legally registered name and had a certificate to prove it.

When mama looked at his certificate and still, to her surprise, it read Sylvester.

When questioned, Sylvester told mama he had no intention of changing his first name, that it was his second name he didn't like.

His birth name was; Sylvester Bud Savage. The official change read; Sylvester Burt Savage.

When asked why he changed his middle name to Burt, he replied that he really liked Burt Reynolds as a actor and wanted his name to be Burt also!!??

I have concluded that America's greatest enemy is ignorance and poverty, so brace yourself for this one!

Sylvester had a neighbor friend who lived next door, who was both a Baptist Preacher and a full time employee of the Atlantic Coast Line Railroad.

As a matter of fact, Sylvester pulled a few strings to get the preacher his railroad job and he was most appreciative.

The preacher had lived next door to my parents for about five years, when he and his family went on vacation out of state.

A few days after the preacher and his family had departed, Sylvester noticed a large U-Haul Truck parked in the preacher's driveway.

Sylvester walked next door to the preacher's house and noticed four men loading the preacher's furniture onto the truck. When Sylvester asked the men what they were doing, they replied that they were moving this family up north.

Sylvester told the men that his neighbor had said nothing about moving or leaving his railroad job, that he thought the preacher was on vacation.

The four men told Sylvester that all they knew was that this family was moving and they had been hired to load everything in the house.

They also told Sylvester to mind his own damned business and to leave them alone and let them do their job!

Not wanting to offend the four men further, Sylvester apologized and then walked back over to our house and told mama to fix the men a large pitcher of iced tea.

Returning to the preacher's house, Sylvester brought the pitcher of tea and four glasses to the men. He then remained with them, holding the doors open and helping them to load everything from the preacher's house onto the truck.

When the movers had finished their work they thanked Sylvester for his help and drove away. The house was completely empty to include all the furniture, appliances and articles of clothing.

Sylvester locked up the empty house and returned to tell mama that everything was gone and that he couldn't understand the preacher moving away, leaving his good railroad job and deserting his church without telling anyone!

Well I guess you've figured this one out by now, because the preacher returned home a few days later finding his house completely empty.

Knocking on our front door, the preacher asked Sylvester if he had seen any strangers over at his house while he was on vacation?

Sylvester replied; "Only the movers with their U-Haul!"

The preacher then explained to dumb-ass Sylvester, that those men weren't movers, they were burglars and they had stolen everything they owned!

The preacher was astonished to learn that Sylvester not only provided the burglars with ice tea, but that he had actually helped them to load the truck as well!

I really felt sorry for the preacher and his family... but I felt more sorrow for Sylvester's ignorance.

Sylvester buys a TV:

The Savage house never had a television and I can remember mama pleading with Sylvester for a year to buy one for us children.

Sylvester kept saying that television sets were nothing but trouble and he wasn't going to put out that kind of money when we could get by without one!

In time, mama somehow convinced him and announced that Sylvester was going to buy us a TV.

Instead of buying a new model, he let some ignorant, coon-dog chasing, red-neck, son-of-a-bitch who worked at the railroad yard, talk him into buying his old junky TV with a frigging coat hanger for an antenna. Sylvester said he got a good deal at fifteen-dollars!

Sylvester brought that worn-out piece of shit home, plugged it in the outlet, turned it on and started cursing! All we got was a screen full of snow and even that was flipping like crazy.

Twisting and turning every knob and button he could find, Sylvester finally jerked the plug out of the wall and started screaming; "I told you these damn things weren't worth a shit, but you kept insisting that I buy one." ..."This no account bastard won't work and now I might not get my fucking money back!" "Fuck all of you and your damned television!"

That was the first and last television set I ever saw, until I was grown, married and had a family of my own!

SYLVESTER'S REVENGE

Sylvester was an addicted philanderer. There was absolutely nothing he could do about his whore-mongering ways. He was absolutely obsessed with his cravings for the female anatomy.

Sylvester used up mama by pumping six babies into her belly, none of which he ever planned or wanted.

He never used birth-control and absolutely refused to ever use a condom. He used to make the statement; "having sex with a condom, is like washing your feet with socks on!" Sylvester said he liked the feel of flesh against flesh and that any man who screwed his wife with a rubber was a sissy!

That's why mama had six children back-to-back and the same reason my father brought home a venereal-disease and gave it to mama without any concern for her health.

Sylvester knew he had acquired VD and wasn't man enough to tell mama. He took a weeks vacation and told her that he was going to Tennessee on vacation to see his relatives. Where he was really going was to check into a hospital for venereal-diseases and get his ass cleaned up, leaving mama to fend for herself.

Mama not knowing that Sylvester had transmitted VD to her, broke out with a rash and then what looked like measles. It took this break-out for mama to go to a doctor and discover that she in fact had a case of VD!

Mama and Sylvester were both cured and as a defense, Sylvester had the gall to accuse mama of giving him the disease. That's a good illustration to show just how sorry and ignorant he was!

As for the six children that Sylvester produced, there was never one occasion where he took any one of us to a sporting event, a fishing trip, never a concert, a carnival or circus, never attended any of our school activities, never took time to go to even one little league ball game to see his boys play, not even so much as a night out for a movie!

There were two reasons for this; one was that he didn't want to spend any of his money to entertain his children.

The second reason was obvious; he never wanted any of us in the first place, so why would he find pleasure in spending time with us?

Here's a good example to show how Sylvester protected his precious money, that he never shared with his wife or children:

Just out of the service, I remember clearly one afternoon that I was stranded on the side of the road. My car ran out of gas and I didn't have any money or a credit card on me.

I spotted Sylvester's car heading in my direction on his way to work. When I flagged him down, he rolled down his window and asked me what was wrong. I told him that I was out of gas and didn't have any money on me. Sylvester replied; "that's too bad son!" ... and drove away!

Another example happened one Saturday morning when Sylvester got up on a step ladder in the hallway of our house. Above his head was a cut-out removable panel which provided access to a small attic.

Sylvester asked us kids for help in removing several large, old metal ammunition boxes. The boxes were extremely heavy because they were full of silver dimes. Sylvester had been stashing the silver dimes in the boxes for many years and nobody but him knew it!

Sylvester asked us to help him count and wrap the silver dimes, which we did. By the time we finished rolling the dimes there was more than four-thousand dollars. We tried to explain to Sylvester, that the silver content of the dimes was far more valuable than the face value. At that time, the silver value was about three-times face value.

Sylvester didn't seem to comprehend what we were telling him and kept bragging that he'd now have enough money to pay off his Cadillac in full.

About a week later, Sylvester came home bragging to mama that he now had a clear title to his Cadillac. He had swapped the rolled dimes for a paid in full receipt for the three-thousand nine hundred dollars balance he owed on his car.

Mama asked Sylvester if he swapped the rolled dimes at face value for the car title?

Sylvester replied that he had! Until he died, he never comprehended that he gave the credit union more than double the face value of his dimes to pay off a four-thousand dollar note!

Who knows what collector value there was as well??!!

Sylvester always hoarded his money unless it was for something he desired, such as his women.

Any member of the Savage family would tell you that Sylvester put away fifty-cents of every dollar he made. It was estimated that when he died, there was more than one-hundred-thousand dollars in cold cash stashed away in some secret hiding place.

He could have buried the money on his property, stashed it inside the walls of the house, hid it in the attic... who knows?

Sylvester hid his money because he never fully trusted banks, savings or credit unions, since the great-depression. He was certain that another great crash was coming!

The problem with this was that Sylvester didn't trust his wife or any of his children either. He never confided in anyone about his secret hiding place and never made a will, because he was certain that he would out live mama and everyone else. Sylvester thought that he'd live forever and nobody, but nobody was going to get their hands on his money!

Sylvester needed a hip-replacement and was scheduled for surgery. I was visiting mama when he asked me to drive him to the drug-store to get his prescription filled. This was just weeks before his surgery and his unexpected death!

While driving Sylvester to the drug-store, I asked him if he had taken the time to draw-up his will. I told him that both he and mama at their age should have already taken care of this responsibility.

Sylvester looked me straight in the eye and responded; "don't you worry about me or my will son!" "I've taken care of everything and I expect to be around for many years to come!"

Weeks later, Sylvester was dead within hours after his hip-surgery. He died without a will. Mama didn't even know where Sylvester's important papers were, such as his car-title, bank-statements or insurance policies.

Only God knows to this day, where he hid his cash savings. He did a good job, because it has never to our knowledge been found!

My only sister Betty, believed till the day she died, that our brother Harold found Sylvester's hidden cash and kept it for himself.

After Sylvester passed away, Harold spent several days searching the entire house, to include attics, closets and walls.

Another reason why we suspected Harold of finding the cash and telling mama that there was nothing there, was because he did a similar thing with my grandma's house when she died.

A few years earlier, grandma had suddenly died of a heart attack. Harold jumped in his station-wagon and drove to grandma's house and looted everything of value to include all her antiques.

There were some very valuable things in grandma's house such as an original pendulum Coca Cola School Clock, my grandpa's antique double-barrel shotgun and some priceless collectibles.

Harold looted everything and took the valuables to his home.

Not one of the other grandchildren received anything from grandma's old house. Mama got the empty house which was next to worthless. Mama loved Harold so much, that she said nothing about what he had done and told the other grandchildren that she was sorry we missed out!

One thing for sure, old Sylvester got in the final blow of revenge by leaving mama in one hell of a mess with no will and no idea where he hid his savings. Mama would have a terrible time trying to convert his personal property over to her name. She spent months with lawyers and in court searching for documentation or any liquid assets that may have existed.

Mama would come to learn later, that Robert knew all the time where Sylvester hid his important papers. With the point of a finger, Robert could have revealed all of Sylvester's valuable paperwork, but he didn't. Robert had his own reason for keeping quiet... but that's another story!

Mama was left with virtually nothing from Sylvester's estate and has continued to survive on her own small pension from the telephone company.

Even in death, old Sylvester got his revenge against mama.

Rest in peace Sylvester.

THE WRATH OF
SYLVIA "MA-BARKER" SAVAGE

Mama has on occasion been jokingly referred to by some family members as; Sylvia "Ma-Barker!" Savage.

The real Ma-Barker was a famous "Tommy-Gun" toting, female shoot-um-up gangster from the 1920s.

Sylvia Savage is a Christian lady, who spent her entire life loving and protecting her children. She was so protective of her children, that she wouldn't even allow us go swimming with our friends, because she was afraid one of us would drown.

We would beg and plead with mama to let us go swimming, where she would always reply: "I'll never let you to go swimming until you learn how to swim!" Try making logic out of that statement.

Mama grieved for her children growing up with less than the bare necessities of life, while her husband screwed around and spent a good portion of his salary on every available skirt within fifty miles of our house.

Mama loved the Lord with all her heart. However, on occasion her Christian manner and language would alter, due to the hell on earth that she lived in with my father. She would explode in anger over some of Sylvester's antics and would attack him verbally with some very strong explicit phrases, not suitable for Sunday morning worship! Later, after a cooling down period, mama would pray to the Lord for forgiveness.

Sylvester tried to cover his tracks and thought he'd never get caught with any of his women. Since he never allowed mama to have any modern appliances, like a washing machine, he knew that she was committed to one of two places most of the time.

She was either working her job at the telephone company, or scrubbing the family's laundry on a scrub board in three large galvanized wash-tubs.

Mama had to wash our clothes on the back porch, sometimes in freezing weather.

Mama always wanted an electric washing machine with a wringer attachment on top, but a washer was out of the question.

I can still see mama scrubbing the family wash with her barehands on a wash board. Her knuckles would bleed from rubbing the clothes on the galvanized ridges of the board, especially during the winter months when her skin would develop cracks from the cold.

Mama still cooked on an old kerosene stove and made our toast on a metal device that sat over the flame, where you could place one slice of bread on each side.

We didn't have a refrigerator like our neighbors. We had what was called an "Ice-Box", where a block of ice had to be inserted.

I remember an old black man we called "Shorty", would pull up to our front door every other day with a mule drawn wagon loaded with large blocks of ice. Shorty would charge us twenty-five cents for a thirty pound block of ice. He would carry it into our house on his shoulder, which he had padded with a croaker-bag made of burlap material.

The folded croaker-bag absorbed the water drippings and provided some cushion from the weight of the ice for Shorty's shoulder bone.

He would use an ice-pick to chip away at the block of ice, until it would slide into the top compartment of our ice-box.

We could never keep any meat in our ice-box, because there was no way to freeze or preserve it. If mama cooked any meat, it had to be purchased on the day it was to be cooked.

I doubt very seriously if our house could have accommodated any modern appliances anyway, because we still had the old fuse-box that regulated the electrical currents. Sylvester wouldn't spend his money to have the fuse-box replaced with a circuit-breaker.

When our fuses would blow, which was every day, we had to replace the blown-fuse with a fresh one. Sometimes when we ran out of fuses we would carefully slip a copper-penny into the slot behind the fuse, carefully screw the blown fuse back into the slot and presto... we had power again.

God knows, it's a wonder we didn't burn the house down with our direct-circuit antics. How some of us weren't electrocuted while performing this make shift, direct-circuit repair beats me!

Even with our hardships and mama's harsh schedule, Sylvester didn't get away with all of his dastardly-deeds.

Mama was a better detective than "Sherlock Holmes", because she had a special knack of knowing when and where Sylvester was playing around!

I never understood how she could know, but she did keep track of Sylvester and his whores, as she called them!

Mama could give a shit who Sylvester was sleeping with, but when it came to taking food off her children's table she would come unglued.

Mama knew he was spending money on flowers, candy and gifts for his women, so when mama hit the boiling point we knew that all hell was going to break loose and that somebody was going to suffer dearly! On a number of occasions, Sylvester really paid the price for his running around.

Example #1: (Sylvester's Bathrobe Ordeal)
My father worked nights at the railroad, so he slept during the daylight hours. While he was sleeping one day, mama opened the trunk of his car and found a gift wrapped box.

I was only six years old then, but I remember mama was very quiet when she carefully opened the gift box and found a new lady's bathrobe.

Mama wrapped the box back to it's original condition and placed the gift box back in the trunk of Sylvester's car.

She told me to keep it a secret and not to let my father know that we found the box. At the time, I assumed the gift wrapped box to be a gift for mama, since it was a lady's bathrobe. I don't know what made me think this, because my father never bought mama any gifts!

When my father got up from his sleep, he bathed, got dressed and walked out the front door. Mama took me by the hand and we hurried into the front room and peeked out the window to see what my father would do.

To show you how ignorant he was, he removed the gift wrapped box from his trunk, tucked it under his arm and started walking up Edison Avenue, the street where we lived.

Still holding my hand, mama hurried out the front door and carefully looked up the street to see where my father was going. It's obvious to me now, that mama already knew my father was having an affair with a woman who lived a few blocks further up Edison Avenue.

My father entered the front door of a house, just like he lived there.

Still holding my hand, mama hurried up to that house where my father was and told me to stand where I was on the sidewalk until she came out. I stood there like some statue not knowing what was going on!

It was less than a minute, when I heard all kinds of screaming and cursing, as mama came backing out of that house dragging some woman by the hair on top of her head. The woman was bent over as mama continued to pull her out of the house onto the front porch.

That's when mama started to slap the woman on top of her head with her right palm, while holding the woman's hair with her left hand.

Mama must have slapped the top of that woman's head ten or fifteen times as hard as she could. I know that it must have hurt her hand about as much as it hurt the woman's head.

Mama knew exactly what she was doing when she dragged that woman outside on the front porch.

She knew that all the screaming and cursing, which mama was doing most of... would bring all the neighbors out on their front porches.

Mama wanted all the neighborhood to see just what they had for a neighbor and wanted all the world to know one more time that Sylvester was still a no good whore-mongering son-of-a-bitch!

After the one sided fight ended, mama took me by the hand and shuffled her way back home, pulling me behind her like a rag doll!

Example #2: (Sylvester's Affair with his brother's wife)
Sylvester had a brother who lived in Tennessee. Mama knew that Sylvester had on occasion slept with his brother's wife. She didn't worry herself too much, because she knew that Sylvester only made one visit a year to Tennessee on his vacation. My parents never took a vacation together during their sixty-years of marriage.

Sylvester's brother Albert never knew his wife was having a sexual affair with my father, because Albert was a strong Christian man, who trusted The Lord, his brother and his wife completely.

My father was notified by telephone that his brother Albert had suffered a heart attack and was in the hospital. My father saw this as a great opportunity to make an emergency trip to Tennessee... not so much out of concern for his brother's health, but a good chance to be alone with Albert's wife, while Albert was recuperating in the hospital!

Mama knew damned well that Sylvester would use this unfortunate opportunity to lay Albert's wife, so she suggested that my father take me along with him.

Mama was thinking that at six years of age, I would be right under Sylvester's feet all the time and that would reduce his opportunities for any sexual encounters.

This time, she was totally out of the ball-park in her way of thinking. Sylvester wasn't about to allow my skinny little ass to interfere in his romantic escapades.

I remember that we drove to Tennessee and then directly to Albert's house. Albert's wife Velma met us on the front porch as we drove up. After a few hugs and kisses, my father introduced me to her as his youngest child.

My father told me to sit on the front porch swing, that he and Velma had to look for some insurance papers in the house to take with them to the hospital when they visited Albert.

I sat on the porch swing, but could see through the sheer front window curtains. My father embraced Velma and started kissing her full on the mouth. He was groping her body with his hands so hard, that he would have received an Academy Award for porn, if I could have caught this scene on tape!

As I think back, in those days, there was no such thing as Video Recorders or even 8MM Cameras.

After five minutes or so, my father came out the front door with Velma, who was carrying a small suitcase.

Now here is what he said to me:

"Johnny, we're going to drive over to the hospital, which is about thirty miles from here!"

"We're going to stay over there for two or three days, until my brother's health improves."

My father then told me that I couldn't go with him and that I was going to stay with one of my cousins whom I had never met.

I was only six years old and didn't want to stay with some

cousin I'd never met. My father never bought any of his children pajamas, so we had to sleep in our underwear. This would be embarrassing to stay in a house with people I didn't know.

It didn't matter. My father wasn't going to miss the opportunity to travel to another town and spend the night with his brother's wife.

There was no way he was going to drag me along to screw up this opportunity for him to put another notch in his whore-mongering belt!

My father pointed at a house about half a block down the street and said: "you have a cousin that lives in that house and when she and her husband come home, they'll come up here and get you!"

"I'm going to leave a note on their front door, that you're sitting here on the front porch!"

I asked my father and Velma, if I could stay in the house, because it was cold on the porch. I remember it was late fall and in Tennessee the nights get very cold that time of year.

My father said that I had to stay on the porch, because Velma didn't want to leave the house unlocked with just me there!

I'll never forget as long as I live, my father and Velma driving off into the sunset, leaving me there on that front porch with my little suitcase.

I sat there on the porch swing hour after hour. The last time I had anything to eat was breakfast early that morning. Darkness fell and with it came the bitter cold.

It was about 1:00 A.M., when I saw a car headlight turn into the driveway of my cousin's house. I sat there for a few more minutes until a man and woman walked up and asked me if I was Johnny?

The woman introduced herself as my cousin Nell and her husband's name was Stud. She said that I could come to their house and stay with them.

Even though it was strange to stay in a house with people I didn't know... it sure beat sitting on that front porch in the cold any longer.

I slept in my clothes, because I was embarrassed to sleep in my underwear in a strange house with strange people!

During the time I was there, my cousin called my aunt Lula, who I'd never met either. My aunt was informed of my situation and told what my father and Velma had done to me.

I didn't know until later, but aunt Lula was my father's half-sister, who had the temper of a wildcat. She would tell it like it is and it didn't matter to her who liked it or not! She knew exactly what was going on between my father and Velma!

I stayed with my cousins for three days, until my father and Velma came back.

My father called aunt Lula and wanted to visit with her and introduce her to his youngest son.

Aunt Lula told my father to come on out to her farm and to bring Johnny and his suitcase with him.

When we arrived at aunt Lula's farm, she told me that I was going to stay with her until my father's vacation was over.

I remember that she was so good to me. She let me ride one of her horses every day and she cooked great country meals for me.

My father didn't fare so well. Aunt Lula lit into him with the fury of hell and in no uncertain terms expressed her anger about his leaving me on that front porch swing for eleven hours in the winter cold, just so he and Velma could have a sexual rendezvous at some cheap motel.

Before we departed Tennessee to return home, my father's brother died. We attended Albert's wake and funeral which I knew little about. I had heard of a funeral before, but knew nothing about any wake.

The only thing I remember was... that Velma's husband was on display in the living room of his home for several days.

Nobody, including me, got more than a few hours sleep during this thing they called a wake!

My father's troubles didn't end when we drove away from Tennessee.

When we finally arrived back home in Jacksonville, Florida,

mama was waiting for him! It seems that aunt Lula had called mama while my father and I were driving home and told her about Sylvester's decision to dump me in a cold strange place alone and drive away with his brother's wife.

Sylvester caught some kind of hell for his actions and mama didn't soon let him forget what he did.

Some of the things that mama said to my father aren't suitable for print!

Example #3: (Thanksgiving Dinner)
It was Thanksgiving day and mama had cooked a beautiful dinner for the family. Since mama was working and had her own money, we ate much better than before she went to work.

I was about twelve years old then and I can remember we had the traditional turkey, dressing, mashed potatoes, green beans, candied yams, cranberry-sauce, hot rolls, salad and dessert.

We all pigged-out, including my father, who had a couple helpings of everything.

After dinner, my father got all dressed up in his suit and tie, told mama that he had some errands to run and drove away in his Cadillac.

Mama was very calm for about thirty-minutes, then she called her friend Mrs. Wilkins to drive her somewhere. Since mama didn't drive, her friends would sometimes take her places, if it was convenient for them.

Mrs. Wilkins picked mama up at the house and they drove away. I thought they were going shopping for some Thanksgiving sales or something.

Somehow mama knew that her beloved husband was romancing one of his whores at the Piccadilly Cafeteria across town.

When mama and Mrs. Wilkins arrived at the Piccadilly Cafeteria parking lot, they spotted Sylvester's Cadillac. He was there!

Mama told Mrs. Wilkins to follow her into the cafeteria, to go through the food line, to fill her tray with a complete Thanksgiving dinner and that mama would pay for it.

Mrs. Wilkins said to mama; "Sylvia, I can't eat another Thanksgiving dinner, I just finished one less than an hour ago at home!"

Mama assured Mrs. Wilkins that she wouldn't have to eat the dinner, but to do what she asked of her!

By this time, mama had spotted Sylvester sitting at a romantic booth with his whore, eating another Thanksgiving dinner.

After mama and Mrs. Wilkins had filled their trays with food, they walked over to the booth where Sylvester and his whore were sitting.

Mama slid into the booth next to my father, while Mrs. Wilkins slid in next to Sylvester's woman.

Now here they are, all four sitting in one small booth, with my father and his woman sandwiched-in between mama and Mrs. Wilkins.

Mama said: "Sylvester, how in the hell can you sit there and eat another Thanksgiving dinner when you just got up from our table at home less than an hour ago?"

My father was so shocked and filled with panic, he momentarily was unable to speak!

Mama said; "If you're so damned hungry then you can eat what you have and when you're finished you can eat what's on my tray and Mrs. Wilkin's as well!"

Sylvester said; "hell no I ain't eatin the food on your tray or anybody else's!" … "my friend and I are leaving right now!"

Mama said; "you just think you're leaving you son-of-a-bitch!"

With that statement, mama pulled a Thirty-Eight Special Revolver from her purse and shoved the barrel so hard into Sylvester's gut, that she tore his dress shirt!

Mama then said; "both you and your whore are gonna eat everything on this table or I'll blow your fat ass clean out of this booth!… and when I'm finished killing you, I'm gonna blow a hole in your whore's ass too!"

Now the woman that my father was dating, started to cry and

begged mama not to kill her. The woman told mama that she didn't know Sylvester was married!

Mama said; "shut up and eat, if you want to go on living!"

After Sylvester and his woman finished eating all the food on the table, mama and Mrs. Wilkins got up, shouted a few more obscenities at the romantic couple and walked toward the door.

Mama told the cashier as she was walking out the door that Sylvester would pay the check and pointed at his table.

Once outside in the parking lot, mama told Mrs. Wilkins that she was going to drive the Cadillac home... that she had a spare key in her purse.

Mrs. Wilkins pleaded with mama not to drive the Cadillac home, saying; "Sylvia, you don't know how to drive a car and you don't have a drivers license!"

Mama said; "I don't care, I won't allow Sylvester to drive his whore home in this car... they can take a taxi or walk!"

With that, mama got into the Cadillac, started the engine and drove it home. Needless to say, when she got home, the Cadillac was bent and bruised in several places and mama later had to replace a few mail boxes along the route she traveled!

Example #4: (Scissors Attack)

I was twelve years old, at the house alone late one afternoon when two police detectives rapped on our front door. One man who identified himself as Detective Allen, started asking me questions:

"Is this the Savage residence?" I answered yes!

"Are you the son of Sylvia and Sylvester Savage?" I told him I was!

"Do you know where your mother is?" ... I told him I thought she was at work!

"Do you have a neighbor that you can stay with until your mother comes home?" I told him that I could stay with Mrs. Eldrich!

"Let's go talk with Mrs. Eldrich young man!"

I walked over to the Eldrich house with the detectives following behind.

Mrs. Eldrich came to the door and started talking with the police detectives. They walked out on her back porch so I couldn't hear.

When the detectives walked away, Mrs. Eldrich had tears in her eyes, and said; "Johnny, you stay here with me and Mr. Eldrich until your mama comes home!" She told me that mama would explain everything when she got there!

Two-hours later, mama came home in a police cruiser and walked over to Mrs. Eldrich's house to retrieve me and to explain everything in detail.

Mama didn't keep anything from me, because she knew that I'd soon learn the truth anyway. Here's what it all boiled down to...

Mama somehow knew that Sylvester had found him a new whore and she even knew when Sylvester was to visit her.

Mama went to work that day as usual, so my father thought it was safe to go see his whore. What Sylvester didn't know was that mama didn't really go to work, she only pretended to go.

Mama had made pre-arrangements with her friend Carol to meet her and drive mama to the house where Sylvester's new whore lived, near the intersection of Post Street and Edgewood Avenue.

Mama had Carol circle around the block a couple of times until mama spotted Sylvester's Cadillac parked about one-hundred yards away from the house.

Mama told Carol to let her out of the car and to drive away and not come back!

Carol knew without a doubt, that Sylvia "Ma-Barker" was about to raise hell out of the bowels of the earth and pleaded with mama not to do something that she'd regret the rest of her life!

Mama said to Carol; "I'm going to stop that son-of-a-bitch once and for all from sleeping around on me and spending his pay checks on his worthless whores!"

"My children have too many needs and have suffered all their lives because of Sylvester's skirt-chasing!"

"This will end his bull-shit once and for all!"

Mama got out of the car and started walking toward the house where Sylvester and his whore were believed to be!

Carol drove away crying and shaking like a willow-branch in a storm!

As mama approached the house, she knew in her mind that Sylvester was in there, in bed with his whore, pumping his fat ass away!

To get into the house mama had every intention of kicking the front door open. But to her surprise, found that Sylvester in his eagerness to romp in bed... didn't take the time to lock the front door!

Mama turned the door-knob and walked right in. Creeping quietly down the hall she could hear Sylvester and his woman grunting, groaning, moaning, and sweating away in the bedroom.

Mama quietly sat her purse down on the hallway carpet outside the bedroom door, but not before removing a pair of sewing scissors with nine inch blades!

She gripped the scissors handles in her right hand and kicked the bedroom door as hard as she could. The door flew open, and Sylvia "Ma-Barker" went to work on Sylvester's ass!

Sylvester was laying butt-naked on top of his naked whore when mama made her first swing with the scissors.

The first blow entered Sylvester's back, where the blades were buried all the way to the scissors handles.

Without slowing her pace one bit, mama slammed the scissors blades into Sylvester's body thirteen additional times, striking him all over the back and front sides of his body as he tried to turn and defend himself.

There was no defense options for Sylvester! The blows were so traumatic that he was zapped of all his strength after the first two or three stabs.

After fourteen total stabs, mama thought Sylvester was dead for sure.

The naked whore as mama called her was now screaming and begging for her life, as mama turned her attention toward her.

Mama chased the naked woman through her own house until she caught up with her in the living room. As mama started to swing the scissors at the woman, she was stopped in her tracks.

As mama told it later, the woman was so hysterical and frightened, that her adrenaline was flowing like water passing through a garden-hose. As a result, the woman had super human strength!

The naked woman had grabbed both of mama's wrists and as mama described it… "It felt like my wrists were squeezed in a vice, almost to the breaking point!"

The woman eventually released her grasp of mama's wrists and ran out the front door screaming… running naked down the sidewalk to a neighbors house.

When mama turned around to once again focus her attention on Sylvester, she saw that he was crawling down the hall on all fours, leaving a bloody-trail and looking like a slaughtered hog!

Mama stood there watching as Sylvester crawled out the front door, across the front porch and tumbled down the front stairs onto the sidewalk. Bleeding like a slaughtered hog, he passed out.

By this time, quite a crowd had gathered. Those that weren't already outside, were looking out their front windows to see what was going on.

Mama knew by this time, that for sure, someone had called the police. She sat down in a rocking chair on the front porch of that woman's house, rocking away with the bloody scissors in her lap, and waited until the police arrived!

Mama was certain because of the massive quantity of lost blood, that Sylvester was dead and not just passed out. Sylvester by some miracle survived!

Emergency room physicians said that Sylvester's survival was due to his excess body fat which absorbed much of the blows and kept the scissors blades from severing any vital organs or arteries.

I remember that my father eventually left the Intensive Care Unit, but remained hospitalized for weeks.

I know, there is a living God... and I know He protected my mama.

Sylvia "Ma-Barker" was never charged with any crime or offense and the police detectives protected her by somehow silencing this newsworthy event from the media!

MOVING MAMA TO ATLANTA

Mama was in her late sixty's and still living in hell with Sylvester.

All the children were grown and on their own.

Raymond and I were living in Atlanta, Georgia with our families. Robert had also relocated there and had his own apartment.

We worried so much about mama living alone with Sylvester and could only imagine the misery that she was going through.

After many telephone conversations with her, we decided that enough was enough. We set out to convince her to move to Atlanta, get out of her miserable situation and live in peace near her children.

Mama finally agreed that she should be able to live out her life in peace and preserve what was left of her sanity.

My brothers and I started looking for a really nice apartment near us, in an adult community. We found the perfect place for mama to live and secured the apartment with the necessary payment of the first and last months rent and security deposit.

Sylvester had retired from the railroad and was working as a security gate guard at the Jacksonville Farmer's Market. While he was working one day, we made our move.

We loaded-up her bedroom, other miscellaneous furniture, her clothes, personal possessions and headed for Atlanta.

When Sylvester came home from work, mama was gone. As Sylvester would later say to the neighbors; ..."Sylvia blinded me with ass!" (Implying that all he could see when she left was her back-side!)

Mama was settled less than a week, when she called me and dropped a "bomb-shell" in my lap! I'll never forget her words: "Johnny, I want to go back to my own house!"

After catching my breath, I asked her what in the world she was talking about. I reminded her that she was now living in peace and quiet, free of intimidation and mutual hatred between her and Sylvester!

Mama was crying when she made an attempt to explain her reasons for wanting to move back to Jacksonville.

Mama explained that she didn't feel secure in her new apartment like she did in her own home. That she had bought and paid for her home with sweat, blood and pure hell and that she wasn't about to allow Sylvester's fat-ass to take it over and parade his whores in and out at his pleasure.

Mama declared that she wanted to live out her senior years and to die in her own house and her own bed and not in some strange city that she had never visited before.

Mama said: "why should I be forced to move and live in some apartment, when I bought and paid for that house? What right does Sylvester have to take over my home, that he never invested a penny in?... The same home where he tried to starve me and you children out of thirty-five years ago?"

Mama then said: "I'll throw his fat-ass out of that house, but I'm going home and take control of my possessions!"

Needless to say, we moved mama back to her home in Jacksonville, forfeiting the pre-paid rent and security deposit. Mama still lives there and vows to go meet her maker from right there!

Sylvester somehow talked mama into letting him remain, pleading his old age and health.

Robert became so upset about all this that he started to consume volumes of alcohol. He finally reached a point that Raymond and I were going to jointly sign to have him committed to a detox-center where he could be dried out.

Knowing that Raymond and I were serious about our plan to save him, Robert started making calls to mama, begging and pleading with her to stop us from committing him.

Mama told Robert to quietly pack everything he owned and come home to Jacksonville to live with her.

Robert moved out at night on a week-end, before Raymond and I knew he had gone.

He moved back in with mama, where he has remained for twenty five years.

He has never touched another drop of alcohol since his return to Jacksonville.

It was really a tough decision to move mama back into her home with Sylvester. With his part-time job as a security guard, we knew he carried a gun. We also knew that mama always kept a loaded gun in her bedroom.

If mama and Sylvester should get into one of their wars and "Ma-Barker" should surface, then one of them was sure to die of gunshot wounds, if not both of them!

With Robert living there, he may be in a position to head off such a catastrophe.

If we accomplished nothing else in all this, Raymond and I scared the shit out of Robert and eliminated his dependency on alcohol!

HAROLD SAVAGE AND HIS RICH WITCH

When Harold was in his teens, he was a great guy. He loved his mother and he was very kind to his brothers and sister.

Harold also possessed a super talent as an artist. His drawings wouldn't have taken a back seat to Norman Rockwell's works.

The problem is, Harold never did anything with his artistic talents, so nobody but family and friends had the pleasure of his work.

He would draw or paint for his friends, but never went professional.

Many of the cocktail lounges in north Florida had a piece of Harold's art hanging behind the bar, because he frequented watering-holes often. God what a waste of talent!

Harold, like the rest of the Savage children, would do about anything necessary to get out of the Savage household, so he joined the Army Air Corps at age seventeen.

He only served about fifteen months before he was discharged under hardship conditions, due to the Savage family troubles.

After Harold's discharge, he worked in a gas station and helped mama as much as he could on minimum wages for about one year.

He was fortunate to get hired on with the Atlantic Coast Line Railroad as an Engineer trainee.

Most of the Savage men did work for the railroad at one time or another, to include; Sylvester, Harold, Billy, Robert, my brother-in-law Warren and myself.

While working at the railroad yards in Jacksonville, Harold used to frequent a small cafe on the property, where he met a homely waitress named Agnes. Harold started dating Agnes after he found out that she was soon to inherit a large sum of money. He could overlook her looks, if the price was right!

Harold was twenty-one, very handsome and very much a ladies man. Agnes on the other hand was a good twenty years Harold's senior, with pre-mature balding.

When she laughed it was very loud, boring, phony and obviously forced.

I mean no disrespect, but to see Harold and Agnes together was such a contrast, that it looked like Clark Gable dating The Bride Of Frankenstein.

The more he found out about the fortune Agnes was to inherit, the more alluring she became. Harold wasted no time in proposing marriage.

This caused a great turmoil with mama and my grandma, because of the contrast in age and appearance. Grandma called Agnes, "Harold's Old Rich Witch" and she really made him mad when she asked him; "why do you want to marry an old woman?"

Agnes was still capable of bearing children and that was important to both mama and grandma. However, their earlier attitude and opinions established a life long barrier between Harold, Agnes and the Savage Clan.

Because Harold was so handsome, he knew that Agnes wouldn't turn down a marriage proposal. They were soon wed, but that didn't prevent him from cheating on her from the day they were married till five-years before his death.

Harold fell into a financially secure lifestyle that was beyond his most vivid expectations. He bought all the things that he had only previously dreamed of, to include a new home, swimming pool, cars, boats, motorcycles and the like.

Because of his sudden financial windfall, Harold felt the need to protect his financial assets. Both Harold and Agnes decided it best to declare his blood family as non-existent. There was a fear that sooner or later some of his family may ask for a loan or some other financial favor. Before that happened, they decided to just get rid of all of us.

All of the Savage clan was so informed that Harold was ashamed of his old family and none were welcome at his new home or in his swimming pool.

Harold then declared that both his mother and father were dead and continued to repeat this for the next thirteen years. For all that time, he never once called or stopped by their house, even though he lived only four blocks away!

Harold and Agnes eventually had two daughters, who were later told that their grandparents were dead, that both were killed in an automobile accident.

I can understand Harold's feelings of insecurity and a need to protect his assets, but how in the hell that man could live four blocks from my parents house and not once in thirteen years bother to call or visit his mama is beyond my comprehension.

This was most devastating to his precious mother, who never did anything but love, protect and sacrifice her life for him.

During Harold's thirteen-year absence his sister Betty died.

Betty's oldest daughter made the mistake of calling Harold to inform him that Betty had died of cancer. Harold's reply to the news was; "what in the hell do you want me to do about it?"... Naturally, he didn't attend his sister's funeral!

Try to picture this; thirteen years after Harold and his witch declared his family deceased, mama and Sylvester were raking leaves on their front lawn. Sylvester spotted two teenage girls walking up the street toward the house.

Although no one-on-one contact had been made in the past

thirteen years, he knew that the two young girls were Harold's daughters.

As the two girls walked past my parents house, Sylvester spoke to them saying; "I bet you girls have been around at the shopping center and are on your way home?"

The older of the two girls replied; "yes sir we have!"... "how did you know that?"

Sylvester replied; "I know more than that, I know that your names are; Denise & Darla!"

Denise replied; "I don't know how you know that sir, but we aren't suppose to talk to strangers!"

Sylvester replied; "we're not exactly strangers young lady, we're your grandparents!"

Denise replied; "I'm sorry sir, but our grandparents were killed in an automobile accident before we were born!"

Sylvester replied; "I know that's what you were told, but I am your grandfather and this lady standing here is your grandmother!" "Your father is Harold and he's our son!"

The two young girls were frightened and hurried on up the street toward their home.

That evening, both Denise and Darla told their father what happened and what the strange man had said.

Harold admitted the truth to his daughters and told them that as far as he was concerned, his parents *were still dead*. Harold explained that he declared his parents dead after a serious family dispute over thirteen years ago.

Both of Harold's daughters requested permission, on occasion, to visit their grandparents, which he never denied them their right to do!

Two weeks passed by, then one day there was a knock at mama's front door. When she opened the door, there stood Denise and Darla who requested permission to visit.

You can imagine the thrill that mama experienced when she was allowed to hug her two granddaughters for the first time!

Before that visit ended the two girls were very happy to know that they did in fact have real live grandparents.

A bond was established between mama and her two new granddaughters that lives on to this day.

Two years later my father passed away of a heart-attack. Harold got the news from a friend and drove immediately around to mama's house and met her again, after fifteen years of absence.

Harold consoled mama and helped her to make all the funeral arrangements and also attended my father's funeral without one word to other family members.

After the funeral was over, Harold waited a couple of days and then, the real Harold surfaced again!

Harold offered to help mama search the house for my father's money, which we all suspected was hidden there someplace.

All of us estimated that Sylvester had in the neighborhood of one-hundred thousand dollars in cash stashed someplace in that house.

Robert had a secret:
Somehow in the past, Robert had without Sylvester's knowledge, witnessed Sylvester concealing something in a hiding place inside his clothes closet.

When the time was right, with Sylvester out of the house, Robert took a look inside Sylvester's closet and found his very clever hiding place.

The clothes closets in this old house were very small, unlike the walk-in closets of today. When you opened these old closet doors there was one clothes hanging-bar right in your face. You couldn't walk inside if hanging clothes were on the bar!

However, Sylvester had figured out that by backing a few inches inside the closet door and reaching up over the top of the closet door, there was a space of wall about three-feet by three-feet.

Sylvester had taped a large brown envelope to the wall over the door on the inside closet wall. Inside that large-envelope he had his important papers, insurance policy, car-title and five one-hundred dollar bills.

Just looking inside the closet or running your hands through the pockets of suits or other clothing, nobody would ever suspect that anything else was in there. Nobody, but nobody would ever think to back into the closet and look over the top of the closet-door!

Robert decided to share his secret with mama and Harold to save them both time and money trying to locate Sylvester's papers and such.

Robert walked into the kitchen-nook where mama and Harold were drinking coffee and secretly talking about their planned search.

Robert said: "I'd like to ask a few questions and give you some information to help in your search!"

With that, Harold and his arrogant attitude exploded: "Daddy's cash or other belongings is none of your fucking business!"

"So why don't you just get your ass out of our way and let us do what we have to do!"

With that, Robert said: "have it your way, I'm outta here and you can both kiss my ass!"

Harold searched the house and two attic areas for days, before telling mama that there was no money or anything else to be found.

Harold did find out that mama owned one fourteen-acre piece of real estate in Tennessee, which had great value. This property was willed to my parents by aunt Lula (Sylvester's sister) before she died.

Harold somehow talked mama into signing the deed over to him before he drove away. He never returned and never saw his mama again. He died of a heart attack ten years later!

Before Harold's death, during the ten year absence, two of his brothers (Raymond & Billy) passed away. Harold again was notified by his brother Robert, where Harold replied; "that's too bad!"

He then slammed the phone in Robert's ear and again, didn't attend either of their funerals!

The Savage clan all know that Harold ripped mama off for her property and we believed to this day, that he also found Sylvester's stashed loot in the attic.

As for Harold, his funeral consisted of a few friends that worked with him on the railroad, his wife, daughters and sons-in-law. Mama had eye surgery the day Harold died and was too old and sick to attend. Robert and I didn't attend the funeral because we knew that we wouldn't be welcomed. None of the other Savage relatives attended his funeral either.

Agnes had the gall to send mama a cassette recording of Harold's funeral, to show mama that her name was never mentioned even once during the eulogies.

Mama cried for days after Harold's death, because she so wanted to see him one more time. She never dreamed that he would die before her and to this day, she still doesn't understand why he abolished her from his life.

Mama and I listened to the recorded cassette tape and the words spoken at Harold's funeral, to include three eulogies, one of which was from his oldest daughter.

As we listened to the glowing eulogies, we heard how wonderful, kind, caring and giving Harold was. How much he loved his wife, daughters, grandchildren and sons-in-law. How he was loved by all of his friends and railroad workers.

Two former railroad workers praised Harold as the best engineer on the entire railroad system. After forty-nine years of running both freight and passenger trains, that statement was the absolute truth!

However, whoever made the recording of the funeral must have made a mistake, or accidentally erased part of the eulogies. I say this because not once during the funeral did the pastor or any of those giving eulogies, mention any of the following:

* That, Harold had a precious living mother who was nine-

ty-one years of age, who loved him with all her heart and soul and was too old and sick to attend the services.
* That, his mother suffered tremendous hardships in raising, caring and providing for him until he was an adult.
* That, without justification, Harold went a total of twenty-three years without a telephone call or visit to his mother who only lived four blocks away.
* That, Harold told his daughters a lie... that their grandparents were killed in an automobile accident before they were born, and that, the same two daughters found out after they were teens, that they did in fact have living grandparents.
* That, Harold was so loving and caring that he never attended his siblings funerals.
* That, there was no mention during the eulogies of his living brothers.
* That, there was no mention of Harold's illicit affairs with other women throughout his marriage.

Without telling mama, I wrote a letter to Harold's family and requested an updated cassette recording of Harold's funeral. I explained that a good portion of the recorded copy that mama received must have been accidentally erased, because I couldn't find any of these things which I listed.

I never received an updated cassette or an answer to my request!

I never really expected a reply anyway.

May Harold rest in peace!

Concerning Robert's secret about Sylvester's hiding place:
Robert waited until Mama had exhausted every legal means and more than six-months trying to find Sylvester's cash and valuable papers, before he came forward with his story.

Robert told mama how sorry he was that Harold had ripped her off again. Robert also reminded mama of how he had tried to tell her where Sylvester's important papers were hid, but he was cursed at and told to mind his own fucking business!

Now that Harold was gone again, Robert took mama to Sylvester's old clothes-closet, reached inside and ripped the large brown envelope from the inside upper wall.

Mama now had in her hands all the papers that it took six months and much unnecessary legal fees to replace and duplicate. All this still blows my mind.

HAROLD CAUSED A LOT OF ASS-WHIPPINGS

Arriving home daily, from our elementary school, Raymond, Robert and myself, all had specific house chore assignments to complete before we went to bed that evening.

With eight people in our family, mama had to get up early every morning and wash clothes. She washed clothes with a hand scrub-board and rinsed them in large galvanized steel-tubs.

She would then hang the clothes outside to dry.

After washing the clothes, mama would fix us what ever she had for our breakfast. She would get us off to school before washing the dishes and making up the beds.

Mama would work at the house non-stop until it was time for her to walk several miles to work at the Southern Bell Telephone Company.

Mama would be exhausted before ever starting to work on her telephone job!

When Raymond, Robert and I came in from school, it was Raymond's chore to gather the dry clothes off the backyard lines, bring them into the house, fold what he could and then stand behind an ironing board until the balance of the laundry was completed.

Robert and I would clean the house from end to end, sweep, dust and then check the dirt alleys and back yard for paper and debris to pick up.

My brothers and I would then play outside until dark, do our homework while listening to the radio and then go to bed. We had no television or other games to keep us up late.

The last chore that Robert and I had to do before going to bed was to wash and dry all the dishes left over from our supper.

We knew better than to go to bed and leave a pile of dirty dishes in the sink or on the kitchen table. We knew we would face mama's wrath, if she came home to find that mess!

Mama was concerned about the rats and roaches that would crawl out of the woodwork, if we left dirty dishes and food scraps lying about in the kitchen. Not to mention that mama would be extremely exhausted and irritable, after getting off work at 11:00 P.M. and walking home. It would be past midnight by the time she reached the house.

Now for the ass-whippings:

Our older brother Harold, who was in his late teens, would come in late from work, before mama got home and after Raymond, Robert and I had already gone to bed.

Harold would go into the kitchen and fry up a couple of eggs, onion and cheese sandwiches. He would eat the sandwiches; leave the grease soaked frying pan and all the dirty dishes before going out again.

Harold was a night person and ladies man, so he would roam at night after work.

Harold did this time after time after time without waking my brothers and I to clean the mess he left behind.

Now here comes mama in from work. Remember now, she's tired, exhausted and irritable when she arrives home to find this horrible mess in her kitchen with roaches crawling everywhere and me and Robert in the bed asleep.

Without a word, mama would fold a leather belt in half, walk into our bedroom, turn on the light, pull down the covers, drag us out of bed and flail the hell out of our bare, skinny legs, until we thought we were gonna die!

Not knowing why mama was beating us half to death, we could only assume between blows, that Harold had again left a horrible mess in the kitchen.

Mama would scream in our faces that we have chores to do and that she wouldn't tolerate us going to bed and leaving an open invitation for the roaches to invade her kitchen!

We would try to explain that when we went to bed the kitchen was clean.

That didn't seem to satisfy her anger and she would emphasize again, that she had better not ever come home to find this mess or we'd get more of the same.

Needless to say, Robert and I suffered these ass-whippings again and again, while not one word was ever said to Harold about this.

Sylvester would never buy us pajamas, which would have provided some minor protection against the leather belt and our bare legs, so we just had to endure the punishment.

Raymond never got whipped for Harold's antics, because the kitchen-cleaning chore was that of me and Robert. Raymond would just lie still in his bed under the covers not making a sound, while Robert and I got the hell beat out of us.

Thanks for nothing Harold!

ROBERT *"Don't say it like that!"* SAVAGE

My brother Robert is two years older than me. He is a twin to my brother Raymond.

God must have a sense of humor, because when Robert & Raymond were born, there was a vast difference.

Raymond came out of mama looking fat and fit like the "Pillsbury Dough Boy."

Robert came out looking worse than a biology-lab skeleton hanging from a display rack. Robert was very sickly when he was a baby and it was touch and go if he would even survive at all.

Robert's OCD:

Robert developed (OCD) Obsessive Compulsive Disorder prior to his teen years and still today at age sixty-five, he displays some symptoms, but not to the degree that he did as a teenager.

Being raised in the hell we were in, it's a wonder that any of us had any sense at all.

There's no question that Robert's OCD was and is a direct result of the massive abuses that he suffered in his childhood.

Wash those hands:

I can remember some of the disorders that Robert displayed

starting from the age of four. He would wash his hands thirty to forty times a day, until the skin dried out so badly, that his hands would crack open and bleed. Robert's hands were always blood red and so chapped around his knuckles, that they looked burned.

Any minor scratch, cut or sight of blood would put Robert into a frenzy. There could never be any mention of death or anything related to death, in Robert's presence.

Don't step on cracks:
Robert's condition got so intense, that he actually believed the nursery rhyme; *"Step on a crack and break your mama's back!"*

Robert really believed that if he stepped on any crack, he would cause his mama to break her back! He walked around for most of a year on his tip-toes, avoiding every crack in the floors of our old house, as well as those outside on the sidewalks.

He just about drove us all crazy with this shit, until he was finally able to shake this obsession.

Guitar Casket:
I remember that I had a small student guitar I was trying to learn to play. Because the guitar case was lined with a blue felt like cloth, Robert thought the case resembled a casket and every time I opened it, he would start to scream and cry at the top of his lungs. For this reason, I wasn't allowed to practice if he was home.

Because mama wouldn't let me practice, I would get so mad at Robert, I would sometimes lock the bedroom door and play my guitar at full volume, making creepy sounds just to piss him off!

Sylvester on occasion would be in the hall trying to calm Robert's screaming, by banging on the locked bedroom door and shouting; "Johnny, will you please turn off that hell-fire, damn-fire, amplifier?"

My antics usually resulted in a good ass-whipping from mama, but sometimes it was worth the pain.

To keep peace and eliminate future ass-whippings, I finally gave up the guitar.

Show time:
I remember that we were allowed to go to a movie theater once a week on Saturday afternoon. In those days, it cost nine cents for a child to get into the theater for the Saturday matinee.

We got one dime each for the theater, leaving us one penny for a piece of candy. We walked the three mile trip each way to the theater in downtown Jacksonville.

Our brother Raymond rarely made the trip with us, because he knew that trouble and strife was automatic in spending the day with Robert!

All hell would break out when we arrived at the theater complex, because there were three theaters side-by-side, with different movies playing at each and Robert and I never wanted to see the same movie. I loved the macho stuff like horror films with the "Wolfman", "Frankenstein", "Zombies" and "Vampires!"

Robert with his OCD problem couldn't take the fright-films, so he always wanted to go into the theater where musicals or a comedy was playing.

I hated that sissy stuff, so Robert and I would always get into a fight.

I remember once, that we argued over a movie until we got into a fight. Robert finally walked into a musical movie and paid his nine-cents. I had to follow because mama would get mad as hell if I allowed Robert out of my sight.

I paid my nine-cents and as soon as I walked past the ticket-taker, Robert grabbed me around the neck in a head-lock and started punching me in the face.

I defended myself by punching Robert in his face. By this time, the theater manager had both of us by our ears and threw us out onto the sidewalk.

Robert and I both ended up walking the three miles back home without ever seeing a movie and losing our nine-cents.

Robert told mama when we got home and she jumped into the middle of my shit, telling me that if I didn't go to the movie that Robert wanted, then neither of us would be allowed to go at all!

You guessed it... I ended up sitting through hundreds of Fred Astair, Ginger Rogers or Betty Grable movies. God knows, I hated that shit!

Fighting Robert's fights:
Robert's physical stature was frail and weak, making him an easy target for local bullies. Because he was unable to properly defend himself, my brother Raymond and myself would always jump in and fight Robert's battles.

Most of the time, I didn't know who or why I was fighting, just that Robert was helpless and I did what I could to defend him.

You would think that Robert would have been more appreciative of my efforts to defend him as his guardian angel. Not so, he thought because I was two years younger than him and wouldn't hit him back, that he could use me as his personal punching-bag.

Robert was bad about striking me in the face with his fist and running.

I remember once, I was lighting fire-crackers with my boyhood friend Mason, when Robert walked up to me and hit me in the face and started running away.

I had just lit the fuse of a large M-80 bomb, which was the most powerful fire-cracker on the market back then.

The M-80 (which is illegal today) was so powerful that it could blow off the fingers of a child or could destroy a mail-box.

With the fuse burning and my anger boiling, I threw the M-80 bomb in Robert's direction with every ounce of energy that I had.

It wouldn't happen again in a million-years, so I know that God helped me to have my revenge, when that M-80 landed point-blank in the back pocket of Robert's baggy dungarees.

Robert turned the corner running and laughing because he thought he had gotten away with his evil deed. He had absolutely no idea that a burning M-80 was in his back pocket, until the explosion blew the rear-end of his dungarees completely off his frail skinny ass!

Although Robert was hurt and blistered, I never laughed so hard in all my life.

I suffered the wrath of mama later, but if I had it all to do over again, I wouldn't change one thing!

There was another incident with Robert, when mama had Raymond, Robert and myself raking the property around several of the old shotgun houses on our side of the street. We hated this with a passion because it was all dirt, no grass and there was always plenty of trash.

Mama made us do this once a month and always on a Saturday. Our neighbors were just about as trashy as what we were raking and never lifted a hand to help keep the property around their houses clean.

Some neighbors would actually throw their trash off their porches right out on the ground.

There was always soda and beer cans, hamburger wrappers, paper cups, pieces of food and cigarette-butts scattered about the yards.

We would always complain to mama about having to rake not only our property, but the property belonging to two or three other neighbors.

The neighbors and their children would actually sit on their porches and watch us rake and clean their property and then burn it in a big pile after we finished.

Within hours of our labors, those no good S.O.B.'s would start throwing their trash and cans over their banisters again!

Mama tried to explain to us, that our neighbors were sorry excuses for the human race and if we didn't rake the properties and keep the grounds clean, then we would have twice as many rats and roaches as we already had!

I can understand now, just what mama was trying to tell us. However, when you're a small child, who is using six-hours of your Saturday off from school, with no compensation, to rake around two or three houses that weren't even ours, it really starts to piss you off!

As if it wasn't bad enough to rake until I had blisters on both hands, I still had to put up with Robert's shit! He would get tired and then take his anger out on me, when mama wasn't looking.

I remember one day Robert slapped my face and as usual, started to run as fast as he could. Without thinking, due to boredom and exhaustion, I slung my rake by the wooden-handle in Robert's direction, like a big "boomerang".

The rake flipped end-over-end several times before landing with a hard force in the back calf of Robert's right leg.

Five steel teeth of the rake buried deep into the calf of his leg, causing much pain and damage to the leg muscle.

Two hours later, Robert had been to the hospital, had out-patient surgery, Tetanus-shots, bandages and plenty of hugs and kisses from mama.

As soon as mama and Robert returned home from the hospital, you guessed it, I got the living shit beat out of me. My ass was as red as a baboons for about a week.

Robert's food had to be OK:
Robert had another compulsion in that he would never eat anything, before he asked who ever prepared the food the following question; "Is it OK to eat this?"

If the answer was; "Yes!", then Robert would eat. Otherwise he wouldn't eat the food because he thought it was poisoned!

Sometimes one of the brothers would say "No", just to piss him off and get a violent reaction!

OK compulsions grew:
One of Robert's most serious compulsions went like this:

My father worked the night shift at the railroad switching yards from 11:00 P.M. to 7:00 A.M. He would leave the house around

10:30 P.M. As my father made his way to the front door, Robert would be there waiting.

From about age five to at least age nine, Robert had this compulsion where he thought that if his father didn't respond in a certain way, as he was leaving for work, he would be killed at the railroad yards that night.

As my father was walking out the front door, Robert would say; "Bye, see you tomorrow?" and my father must reply; "OK!"

Robert insisted that he repeat this ritual exactly ten times, without any interruptions from the pattern that Robert had established.

If anything disrupted the pattern or one word was spoken out of context, then the process must be started all over. So it went like this:

"Bye, see you tomorrow?" ...."OK!"
"Bye, see you tomorrow?" ...."OK!"
"Bye, see you tomorrow?" ...."OK!"
"Bye, see you tomorrow?" ...."OK!"
"Bye. see you tomorrow?" ...."OK!"
"Bye, see you tomorrow?" ...."OK!"
"Bye, see you tomorrow?" ...."OK!"
"Bye, see you tomorrow?" ...."OK!"
"Bye, see you tomorrow?" ...."OK!"
"Bye, see you tomorrow?" ...."OK!"

Now here is where all hell broke loose! Sylvester was the great intimidator and he would usually do something to cause havoc, unless he was running late for work.

Sylvester would wait until Robert was about half way through with his nightly ritual, then Sylvester would deliberately flare up and shout back at Robert; "OOOOOHHHHH ....KKKKAAAAYYYYYY!!!!!"

Robert of course would go bananas and start crying and screaming at his father; "don't say it like that!" ... "don't say it like that!"

Sylvester would sarcastically laugh in Robert's face and then they would have to start all over again, until it was right!

Sylvester knew damned well that Robert was going to go into a frenzy when he pulled his sarcastic stunt, but he would mess with Robert's head anyway.

Sometimes Sylvester would get mad and just drive away leaving Robert lying on the hall floor crying until he fell asleep from exhaustion.

In Robert's mind, he was certain that his father would be killed at the railroad yards that night, because the ritual pattern was broken. Sylvester never was killed and Robert after a few years outgrew this ritual.

Robert's sanity:

I remember that Robert's OCD problem got so out of control, that mama tried every way possible to get Robert out of the Savage environment, of which she was convinced caused Robert's nervous condition in the first place.

Mama never believed that Robert was mentally ill and still defends that belief today.

Mama begged the Florida Sheriff's Association to allow Robert to become part of the Sheriff's Ranch Home For Troubled Youth, but they refused her request.

Mama found a way to get Robert admitted to the St. Luke's Hospital mental health unit, which was a special home for troubled youth, unlike a regular mental ward for the insane.

Robert stayed there for several weeks and did real well. He enjoyed the peaceful home environment, the understanding and special attention that he was receiving.

What he enjoyed most was the scheduled recreational activities, to include hobbies, crafts and a sports program.

His stay and treatment was cut short because mama could no longer pay for the facility and treatments out of her pocket and Sylvester wasn't about to put out a dime for Robert's mental care!

Robert returned home and his OCD condition re-surfaced it's ugly face once again!

Robert was no teacher's pet:
I can remember a time when Robert was in grammar school and without any visible reason, he'd lay his head on his desk and start to cry.

Robert's teacher who was meaner than the old witch in the movie; "Wizard Of Oz!", would demand to know why he was crying.

When Robert wouldn't tell her, she would punish him by making him lay both hands palm down on the flat surface of his desk, then she would take the sharp edge of a ruler and beat Robert across his fingers and knuckles until they bled!

Needless to say, when Robert got home from school that afternoon, the fury of Sylvia "Ma-Barker" surfaced. Mama took Robert by his arm, walked him back to school, where a war and ass-kicking between mama and Robert's teacher took place.

The principal called the police, who were needed to help pull mama's shoe out of the "old-witch's" ass!

Robert and I were walking to school one morning after all the ass-kicking dust had settled and I asked Robert to tell me why he often cried in school, which caused all this trouble?

Robert confided in me that he'd cry because his mind would start thinking about mama and Sylvester being home alone and he could picture Sylvester beating mama with his fists and nobody there to protect her!

You have to understand that all of us walked off to school at one time or another leaving mama and Sylvester screaming and cursing in each other's face with their fists balled up and ready to fight!

That was enough pressure to devastate the nerves of any elementary school child! Robert was too embarrassed to tell his teacher why he was crying, so he took her ruler beatings instead!

Wouldn't you know it, I was two years behind Robert and

I ended up with that same teacher, who treated me worse than dirt!

She never beat me with her ruler, but she did give me failing grades in every subject and made me repeat the third grade over again, which hurt me very badly and destroyed what little self-esteem I had left!

Robert outgrew many of his childhood OCD problems, but he carried over a few into adulthood.

Robert's fear of funerals:
Robert developed another compulsion, in that he can't stand to attend funerals. Robert is convinced that death germs are floating around in the funeral parlors and that he breathes the germs and they also get on his clothes.

I remember when Robert attended my father's funeral. After it was over he came home and stripped naked. He took his new suit, shirt, tie, shoes, socks, belt and even his underwear out in the back yard of mama's house, put the clothes in a neat pile, poured gasoline all over them and set it ablaze with a match.

There was nothing left but ashes when he finished. One thing is for sure… all those death germs were dead as hell!

Never travel with Robert:
Even as adults, we must be very selective when traveling anywhere with Robert. If he doesn't get you arrested, you can expect at least the possibility of getting into a fight or getting your ass whipped!

I remember once when Robert and I stopped to eat at a Steak-N-Shake Restaurant in Atlanta.

We ordered our meal and were sitting there quietly waiting. All of a sudden we heard a loud crash of dishes hitting the floor in the kitchen. I remember Robert looking over in my direction and saying; "don't worry about a thing… I'll take care of this!"

With that, Robert got up from our booth and walked into the

kitchen. Within a minute, I heard screaming and cursing and shouting of obscenities coming from the kitchen.

A man walked up to the booth where I was sitting and asked me if I was with the idiot, that just walked into his kitchen? I said that I was.

The man identified himself as the manager and ordered me to take Robert and get the hell out of his restaurant.

He had called the police and neither of us was ever allowed to enter the restaurant again! The manager shouted in my face; "your fucking meal wasn't even being prepared in the kitchen. We do our cooking behind the counters on the grill!"

"Now get the hell out of my restaurant!"

I walked outside and waited for Robert, who shortly walked out as well. When I asked Robert what happened, he replied that he went into the kitchen to make sure that none of the broken glass landed in our food and that he and some of the kitchen help got into a fight!

I remember another occasion when I was traveling with Robert and we stopped to eat at a "Big-Boy" Drive-Inn Restaurant, in a south Georgia town. We placed our order and were sitting at the counter when Robert started to question the waitress over and over about the cooks experience.

He didn't want his burger cooked in grease, he had to be sure that his burger was cooked in vegetable oil because of his high cholesterol and on and on and on!!!

Finally, Robert got up and told the waitress that he was going into the kitchen to cook his own burger. This started one hell of a ruckus. The cook ordered him out and threatened to quit his job, if the manager didn't get Robert out of his kitchen.

While all this was going on, some homosexual sitting at the counter kept trying to get me to go into the men's room with him. He told me that he was a famous harmonica player from the old W.C.K.Y. Cincinnati Radio Show in the 1930s & 40s and that he would play me a few songs, if I would just step into the men's room with him!

The manager, Robert, the cook and several other kitchen employees got into a fight. The police were called and both of us were thrown out of the restaurant.

We were provided a police escort out of town and back onto Interstate Seventy-Five, with specific instructions never to return!

I never did get to hear that jerk play his harmonica!

Quality-Inn Or Nothing:

If you can go for days without sleep, then it's OK to travel with Robert. Otherwise stay home!

Robert will only sleep at a Quality-Inn, so be sure that several exist on your travel route or be prepared for some serious sleep deprivation.

Traveling with Robert, I once went two days without sleep, until I passed out at a public rest-area. Robert refused to sleep at any of the hundred or so motels we passed, because they were not a Quality-Inn. Robert is convinced that the Quality-Inn's are the cleanest, most sanitary facilities in America and that other motel chains are infested with germs and bed-bugs.

Robert's love life:

There are so many other incidents to write about, but I must take this opportunity to tell about Robert's love life.

Robert's love life is so bazaar, that even I, who was sometimes an eye witness remain amazed at some of his antics.

Robert has never been and never will be married. He has made the statement many times, that there's not a woman alive that won't jump into the sack with another man, if the right opportunity arises.

He bases this on the fact that of the hundreds of women that he slept with, almost all of them were married.

I asked him once, if he didn't miss having a wife and a family to come home to? Robert made the following comment: "There's not a woman on the face of this earth that I would trust out of my sight!"

"If I was scheduled to get married, my fiancée was standing at the altar in her flowing white wedding gown and Jesus was holding her hand as our best man, I wouldn't believe a damned thing she said!"

You would have to know Robert and the women that have shared his harem. I can truthfully say, that Robert has dated and slept with some of the most beautiful women in the south. He attracts women like flies on honey and gets away with things that seem impossible.

When Robert had his own apartment, he would take one of his beautiful women there and before having sex with her, he would strip her naked, sit her in an empty bath-tub and personally give her a douche.

He kept all the douche equipment in his apartment because he never trusted the women to get themselves clean enough to have sex with him.

Most would sit there and allow Robert to give them a douche while a few rebelled, stating that they had never before in their life been so embarrassed or humiliated. Those few would then leave the apartment and never return. Robert didn't care, thinking they weren't clean enough to have sex with him anyway!

There was seldom dining or entertainment where Robert's women were concerned. It was pick them up, go straight to the douche tub and directly to bed! He must have been a great sex partner because they always came back for more.

If I could bottle what ever Robert's lines were, I would be a millionaire.

I have seen Robert spot a beautiful woman waiting at a bus stop, strike up a conversation and within minutes have that beautiful woman in his car heading for his apartment.

Robert never had a shortage of women. He could pick up his telephone anytime day or night and have one on the way to his apartment within minutes.

I don't know if there were others, but I do know of a waitress named Doreen who worked in a restaurant outside of Atlanta, who gave birth to a baby boy fathered by Robert.

He was working for the railroad at the time and got careless with his fleshly desires, which set him back a few notches.

He did pay for all of Doreen's maternity related costs and provided financial support for her until her baby arrived.

Robert was lucky that Doreen didn't push further for child support. She later married and raised the child in a good home. Robert's son would be in his thirties now.

Robert's extreme jealousy:
There was only one woman in Robert's life, that really captured his heart. Her name was Charlotte and she was the closest thing to being 100% pure, clean and innocent in Robert's mind!

Robert met Charlotte who was visiting Jacksonville at the time and was stunned by her beauty and charm. Charlotte was a nursing student at a college in South Carolina.

Without warning, Robert fell head-over-heals for that woman, who was also likewise attracted to Robert.

When Charlotte had to return to South Carolina, Robert developed a jealous rage that took complete control over his emotions. He just sat around day and night thinking of Charlotte and fantasizing that she might be dating other men or making love to some handsome young college class-mate.

Robert's jealous rage dominated his every thought, until he was driven to spy on Charlotte's activities.

It was a good four-hundred miles from where Robert was now living in Florida, to Charlotte's residence in South Carolina.

Robert would drive this distance about three times a week and sit outside Charlotte's residence in his car to see what time she came home from school.

Robert on occasion would search for Charlotte's car in the college campus parking lots and watch to see if she was walking to her car alone after her evening classes.

Robert made these trips for months, without once telling Charlotte that he was within yards of her on many occasions, hiding and watching her in the darkness from his car. All he really accomplished from these unnecessary trips was an accumulation of thousands of miles of wear and tear on his automobile.

Robert goes into a rage:
The climax of Robert's relationship with Charlotte came to a head when he made an unexpected visit to my apartment in Atlanta late one Friday night.

Answering our front-door, my wife and I greeted both Robert and Charlotte, who were traveling back to South Carolina after a visit to Jacksonville, where Charlotte had relatives.

Robert asked if he and Charlotte could stay the night and rest-up, which was fine with me. We all sat around the kitchen table drinking coffee and talking for a couple of hours.

Since I had to work the next morning, my wife and I bid Robert and Charlotte good night and went to bed. Robert and Charlotte still sitting at the kitchen table, said they would get some sleep after another cup of coffee.

I had been asleep for about two hours, when someone tapped me on the shoulder and whispered ..."Johnny" ..."Johnny"!

Turning my head from a sound sleep, I could see Robert leaning over me and whispering he asked, "where do you keep your bible?"

Knowing that Robert was not and had never been a religious man, I asked him what the hell did he need a bible for at three o'clock in the morning?

Robert responded with; "Charlotte and I want to look up something!" I told Robert where my bible was, rolled over and tried to go back to sleep.

Once Robert left my bedroom, I suddenly realized what he wanted with my bible. When Robert doubted or questioned any of his women, as to their sexual activity while they were out of his presence... he always did the same thing.

He would make his women place their right hand on a bible

and swear before God, that no other man had touched them, had sex with them, or made love to them since he saw them last!

Now this in itself was ludicrous, because most of the women that Robert dated were married and had children. Although good looking, if Robert's women had as many dicks sticking out of them, that had been stuck in them, they would look like a porcupine!

Nevertheless, all his women would swear to God on the bible just to appease him or as mama would say, "to humor him!"

There was no doubt in my mind, that Robert was going to make Charlotte swear on the bible in my kitchen. I was so sleepy, I didn't give a shit what he did, as long as I could get some rest before I had to get up and go to work.

I had barely fallen back to sleep, when I heard what sounded like a bomb exploding in my kitchen.

My wife and I sat straight up in bed, when we heard the kitchen table flip upside down along with flying chairs.

We could hear glass breaking and what sounded like a body hitting the kitchen floor

The noise also woke up my children who were now crying, as well as my sick elderly neighbors in the next door apartment.

I could hear poor-old Mr. Cantwell shouting through the walls, "John, are you all right over there… I'll call the police!"

Mr. Cantwell was about eighty-nine years old and thought I was fighting with a burglar or something because he knew that normally I was a very friendly, quiet and peaceful neighbor.

My wife and I rushed down to the kitchen to find Charlotte lying on the floor in a pile of glass, sugar, coffee and milk. The kitchen table and chairs were upside down and scattered across the room.

I asked Robert what in the hell is going on and he had the audacity to respond with; …"everything is OK… just go back to bed!"

"Go back to bed my ass!"… I shouted back! "You've knocked

Charlotte unconscious and destroyed my kitchen... .and you say everything is OK and to go back to bed?"

I told Robert that the police were on their way and to get his shit together and to get the hell out of my home! My wife and children were trying to get Charlotte on her feet before the police arrived. I could still hear poor-old Mr. Cantwell next door crying out; "are you folks OK over there... is anybody hurt?"

The police arrived and questioned Charlotte about the incident. Charlotte told the police that Robert made her swear on the bible that she hadn't been sleeping with any other men. After telling Robert that she had no other male interests other than him, he attacked her because he thought she was lying!

Charlotte refused to file assault charges against Robert and promised the police that she and Robert would leave town immediately if they wouldn't arrest and charge him with attacking her!

Robert and Charlotte drove away within minutes, leaving me and my wife to clean the kitchen until it was time for me to go to work.

Needless to say, this ended Robert and Charlotte's relationship.

Was Robert crazy?
My father always said that Robert was crazy and when Robert was in his early teens, Sylvester tried to have him committed to a ward for the mentally insane.

Mama told Sylvester that Robert's nervous condition was because of the hardships that Sylvester inflicted upon all of us and that it would be a cold day in hell before she'd allow Robert to ever be committed to any insane asylum.

I guess Robert wasn't as crazy as Sylvester thought, because he finally got the hell out of the Savage house and served four years in the U.S. Navy as a Signalman. He then spent another twenty-years working for the Seaboard Coastline Railroad.

Robert eventually quit the railroad job and moved back home. Twenty-five years later, he still lives with mama.

Robert's only income since moving back into mama's house is a few dollars a day that he makes selling at the local flea-market on weekends. His average daily income is five or six dollars. Robert did start drawing his social security pension three years ago at age sixty-two.

Since living in the house with mama for more than twenty-five years, Robert has little knowledge of the outside world and the changes that have taken place. Unless Robert sees something on TV or hears something at the flea-market he is less informed about the real world than a hermit living in a cave.

Here is a good example of what I'm saying:

When my sister was dying in a north Georgia hospital, I drove mama, Robert and Raymond to see her one last time before she died.

We stopped at a motel to spend the night and next door was a Shoney's Restaurant with the all you can eat breakfast bar.

The next morning we all walked into Shoney's and started through the breakfast buffet line. Raymond was first in line followed by mama, then myself and Robert.

About half-way through the breakfast line, Robert tapped me on the shoulder and asked the following: "how does the cashier know how much to charge?"

He then said; "look at Raymond's plate and mama's plate piled so high and I only have a few things!"

I told Robert that it didn't matter how much he took or what he put on his plate, it was all one price.

Robert replied: "you mean that I can eat anything I want, as much as I want and… it's still all the same price?" I told him that was correct, all one price regardless!

Robert then said; "well how long has something like this been going on, I never heard of anything like this before?"

I told him; "about the last fifteen years at least!"

Robert ate well and learned something new that was going on

while he had been cooped up in his bedroom for the last twenty plus years.

Since Robert has been living with mama, he has no place to take his women. He doesn't make enough money for his own apartment.

All these years, mama has bought Robert his cars, pays for his auto insurance, his medical insurance, his food and even buys his cigarettes.

Mama still gives Robert a few dollars to keep in his pocket for emergencies.

Mama doesn't regret taking care of Robert in a financial manner because he does take care of her, such as doctor visits, grocery shopping, house cleaning, lawn care, etc!

Robert is embarrassed when he meets a woman at the flea-market or when shopping with mama. He doesn't have the financial means or current styled clothes to entertain and no place to take them if he thinks sex is possible.

To cover his lack of success, Robert always blames everything on mama, which is a lie. He tells his women that he was forced to retire from the railroad to take care of mama because none of the other children will help her.

Robert tells his women that he had to sell off his retirement stocks, to care for mama, which is also a lie. He never had any stocks in his life.

In fact, mama sold seven-thousand dollars of her telephone stock and gave Robert the money to go purchase himself a pick-up truck for use at the flea-market. He took the seven-thousand dollars and spent every dime of it at the Greyhound Dog Races.

Mama had to turn around again and purchase Robert a car, which she asked me to do for her. She couldn't trust Robert to use good judgment with that kind of money again. I took the money from mama to purchase Robert a Ford Taurus and handed him the keys. He is still driving that car today.

Many women call mama's house all week long wanting to

speak to Robert. Mama doesn't interfere with his lady friends and is polite, until one occasionally pisses her off!

On occasion, one will verbally attack mama on the telephone by saying that she keeps Robert a prisoner in his own home, that Robert had to sacrifice everything to take care of her.

That Robert can't date or get married, because he must care for mama, bathe her, cook for and feed her, do her laundry and house cleaning!

Mama tells these women, that it's just the opposite. That she has to care for, feed, provide a home, clothes, car, insurance and even spending money, to keep Robert going!

Mama tells these women, that Robert is free to go anytime he so desires, that she can care for herself.

Robert has convinced these women that he is a prisoner in his own home and that mama treats him with less dignity than an animal.

All of which is a total lie, because Robert is totally incapable of providing a living for himself. Without mama, he would be sleeping on the streets!

Mama only has a few years at best to live, because she is now ninety-three years of age. She is so worried about Robert's survival, that she has asked me to assure her, that I'll never allow Robert to go hungry or without shelter. I made mama that promise and I will keep it after she's gone!

Robert actually hides in his bedroom at mama's house because some of his women friends are convinced by Robert's lies that he is in fact a prisoner in his own home.

On occasion, women will drive up in front of the house and park across the street for hours at a time looking over at mama's house.

Others will drive by time and time again all day long hoping to see Robert outside. Most of the time mama is sitting in her rocking chair on the front porch, watching the parade of cars go by.

On one occasion, one of Robert's women parked her van across the street from mama's house and sat there all day long for several days. She would leave after sunset and return the next A.M.

After three days, mama got up from her rocking chair and walked across the street and invited Robert's woman friend to come and sit on the front porch with her.

The woman got out of the van and walked over to mama's front porch and sat down. She introduced herself as Ellen.

When mama asked Ellen why she was sitting across the street for three days, she started to cry and opened up with the following story:

"I love Robert and I feel so sorry for the way you treat him!"

"Don't you know that he sacrificed everything to give up his railroad career and come here to support and care for you?"

"Don't you think that Robert would like a life of his own, a wife and family?"

"You keep him a prisoner in his own home and you verbally abuse him!"

"You probably have him locked up in his bedroom right now because he won't answer the phone and he hasn't been outside for three days!"

Mama listened to all this crap and then asked her if she was through with her speech!

Mama then told Ellen the complete truth about the matter of Robert Savage and how she totally supports him, cares for him, feeds him, clothes him, buys his cars, including the insurance and gives him an allowance so he'll have spending money in his pocket for his cigarettes and snacks!

Mama told Ellen that Robert isn't a prisoner in his own home, because he has never owned a home. That he lives in her home which she has owned for the past fifty-years.

Mama then told Ellen that Robert isn't locked up in his room and never has been.

Mama then said; "as a matter of fact, he's in his room hiding from you right now and refuses to answer the telephone when you call here every day".

Mama told Ellen to go into the house, go to Robert's bedroom and make him come out here on the front porch and tell the truth.

Ellen asked mama if it was really okay to go into the house and confront Robert with what she had said and was he free to leave with her and move in with her?

Mama told Ellen that Robert was as free as a bird, to marry her, to move away, to get his own place, to raise a family or anything else that he wanted to do. Mama said; ..."take him, please!"

Ellen went into the house and knocked on Robert's bedroom door for about fifteen minutes.

When Robert finally did open the door, she told him to pack his clothes, that he was now free to go with her and that his mother gives her blessing.

Robert was now in one hell of a mess! Caught in a pack of lies, he just stood there mumbling like a fool until Ellen realized that everything he had told her was a pack of lies.

Robert didn't leave with Ellen and as she was walking out of the house she told mama that she was so sorry for all the horrible things she imagined about her. Robert had convinced her that he was a prisoner and that his mother was nothing less than a witch!

Ellen told mama that she would never return or call the house again. That was the last mama ever saw of that particular woman.

There have been others before, others since and there will be others in the future, who believe Robert's shit. Mama just laughs about it now and lives her life as best she can. Many women continue to believe mama is a witch out of hell and that poor Robert is her slave and a prisoner held captive in his own home!

Robert can't find work:
It all boils down to this: Robert hasn't had a real job since he moved back into mama's house more than twenty-five years ago.

He doesn't want a job and couldn't survive in the work place anyway. He has been out of touch with the work-force and the real-world far too long.

Robert will tell you that he checks the want ads every day but no one will hire him.

To prove this was bull-shit, I took Robert one day in my car and drove him to a good clean indoor job that I had pre-arranged.

When we arrived, he was hired on the spot and put to work.

I drove away telling Robert I'd be back that afternoon to pick him up.

Less than fifteen minutes later, Robert told his employer that he quit, that he never wanted the damned job in the first place.

He walked off down the street heading for mama's house.

I asked Robert later that day, why he walked off his new job. He replied; "I didn't ask you to find me a fucking job, I didn't know that you were taking me to any fucking job and I don't want any fucking job!" He then told me to mind my own fucking business.

I only did this to prove a point. That Robert was lying when he said nobody would hire him and that he hasn't sought a job nor does he want one.

He'll die like he presently lives, piddling around at the flea-market for five or six bucks a day and watching for the mail-man to deliver his social security check.

Robert has outgrown many of his compulsions, but still today has some that he just can't give up.

Robert's use of paper towels:
Robert will not dry his hands on a cloth towel, in case someone else has used it. He will only dry his hands with paper-towels.

Washing his hands 100 or more times a day, he will go through several rolls every day.

Robert is never without paper towels in his hands. He will pull four or five sheets off the roll each time he dries his hands and then he will pull another couple-sheets to hold in his hands for opening refrigerator-doors, cabinet-doors, house doors, etc!

Mama buys full forty-eight roll cases at a time for Robert at Sam's Discount Store. This will last about two weeks at most.

Robert washes his clothes:
I was visiting mama recently and noticed Robert washing his clothes.

He'll only put one garment at a time in the washing machine, fill it with water, run the full wash and spin cycles, remove the one garment, replace it with another and start filling the machine with water again.

Robert will do this over and over until he has washed all his clothes. Sometimes it takes him half a day.

Robert makes ice-tea:
Robert makes and drinks two-gallons of ice-tea every day. His guts must be as black as the Ace-Of-Spades!

Drinking that much ice-tea is Robert's business, but boiling the tea is another story.

Robert's ice-tea compulsion starts first thing every morning. He will only boil one tea bag at a time.

He puts a small pot of water on the electric-range, brings it to a boil, drops in one tea-bag, simmers and then pours the liquid tea through a paper coffee-filter which has been inserted inside a wire-strainer.

Thus straining his tea into a gallon jug. Keep in mind that he is using tea-bags!

He then puts on another small pot, brings it to a boil and repeats this process over and over until he has made his first gallon of ice-tea. He will make his second gallon later that afternoon using the same process.

Mama said that her electric and water bills run hundreds of dollars each month, but she knows Robert can't control these compulsions, so she just pays the bills and leaves him alone to do his thing!

Robert has little knowledge about the outside world and the

changes that have come about. He was astonished at what he saw recently when he stopped at a rest area on the highway.

"Johnny, you're not going to believe what I have to tell you", he excitedly explained; "when you use the urinal or the toilet, you don't have to put your hands on any filthy handle to flush anymore!"

"Even the sinks are automatic and start running water when you place your hands under the faucet!" Being the hygiene freak that Robert is, he was ecstatic to find out that he never had to put his sterile hands on the commode or sink handles in a public rest room again!

I played along with Robert and acted very surprised at his good news by saying; "you got to be shitting me Robert?"

He soon realized that I was just poking fun at him and got a little annoyed with me.

Robert asked me how long this new invention had been around and couldn't believe it when I told him about the last ten years at least.

I was surprised again recently, when Robert was riding along in my car and made this strange request: "could we stop for some lunch at a Howard-Johnson's Restaurant?" I asked why Howard-Johnson's?

He replied; "because they're clean, give you good portions and have a nice menu selection!"

Robert was shocked when I told him that Howard Johnson's had gone out of business many years ago!

Enough about Robert. He's my only living brother and I love him very much. Other than the things that I have mentioned in this book, *Robert is completely normal!*

RAYMOND SAVAGE

As a child, Raymond was no exception when it came to beatings or abuse. Living in the Savage household and never knowing what crisis was coming his way next, kept him a nervous wreck.

Raymond's nerves caused him to be a habitual bed wetter from about age three to age fifteen.

Every night was the same with Raymond. He would wake up in the middle of the night soaking wet. Mama would have to get up and turn on the light so she could change his bed. Mama's anger would flare, waking everybody out of a sound sleep, causing even more tension.

Mama read in the newspaper where one of the famous traveling Faith Healers was coming to Jacksonville with a tent revival, so she immediately signed Raymond up for a bed-wetting healing!

Raymond was already in his teens and was much embarrassed to go on stage in front of thousands of people for his bed-wetting healing, but he had no choice in the matter.

The healer prayed for Raymond, slapped him in the forehead a time or two and said he was healed.

Mama came home that night proclaiming that Raymond was healed.

Everything might have been okay, but Billy had to start some shit with Raymond before he went to bed, by throwing a full glass of ice-tea in his face, while screaming and cursing him at the same time.

I don't recall why Billy started picking on Raymond that night of all nights. It was just the norm for Billy. I guess who ever was the closest to him when he decided to go into one of his rages became his target!

I do remember that Raymond was so nervous and scared when he went to bed that he pissed like a race horse before morning!

Mama tried to get Raymond back to the healer the next night, but he refused to give Raymond a second slap or even a booster!

Raymond continued his nightly ritual until he was fifteen.

Unlike Robert and myself, Raymond didn't enlist in the Armed Forces when he became seventeen, so he took a lot of the abuses that Robert and I were able to dodge. Being the only teenager remaining in the Savage house was dangerous, but Raymond survived to grow up!

Raymond's First Car:
Mama gets all the credit for Raymond getting his first car. With Robert and I both in the service, mama turned all of her love, attention and protection toward Raymond.

During Robert's four-year tour of duty, he mailed an allotment check to mama every month for safe keeping. She was to put the money in the bank so he would have enough money to buy a car after his discharge.

Returning home with his Honorable Discharge four-years later, Robert asked mama for his bank savings book so he could withdraw his money to purchase his new car.

Like a "bolt of lightning out of hell", Robert heard mama's response: "there is no money, I used it to buy Raymond a car!"

Mama followed with: "he needed a car so he could go back and forth to work!"

Robert went ballistic while Raymond just stood there grinning!

Robert had to watch Raymond drive around in his new car while he rode the bus until he could save enough to make a down payment on his own car! Forty-years later, Robert is still fuming over this!

As an adult, everybody loved Raymond:
Raymond was a beautiful, gentle, humble person and everybody loved him.

A big man who many referred to as a "teddy-bear".

Raymond lived his life expecting to be called any day to fill some big corporate executive position. The call never came!

He worked in retail and wholesale but was never executive material because he lacked the formal education to fill such a position.

Raymond's health and personal appearance had much to do with his failure to land the job of his dreams.

Raymond lived his life on a beer budget, with Champagne taste and big dreams.

At age fifty-nine, he found himself unemployed and in poor health.

He was extremely overweight with a large pot-belly that draped a good eight inches over his belt buckle making it impossible to tuck his shirt-tails into his slacks.

Raymond really tried to find work, but finally accepted the fact that a work career was over. He eventually filed for and received social security disability benefits because of his depression and poor health.

Raymond's obesity was a trait of his family. His only son Charlie virtually ate himself out of the military.

This was the first time in my life that I ever heard of a military man actually eating himself out of the armed forces, but it happened.

It was reported that as a last effort the military sent Charlie to a special fat-farm unit to fight his obesity. During his confinement at this unit, Charlie somehow found a way to call into the city one evening and order a half-dozen large deluxe combination pizzas for delivery.

Charlie and his buddies were caught by the military police where all were later court-martialed and discharged as undesirables.

Most discharged military men return home as heroes to their family and friends who meet them at the air-terminal with hugs, cheers, posters and even the high-school band.

In the case of Charlie, he was sent home by the military the cheapest way possible in the middle of the night on a Greyhound Bus. He was so fat, that the military had to purchase two-seats to accommodate his fat-ass!

His parents were embarrassed when they picked him up at the bus terminal at 2:00 A.M.... but what could they say or do?

Charlie laid around his parents house for months just eating and sleeping between television programs. Charlie loved the pick-up truck commercials where the drivers out west drove their rugged vehicles through the woods, through three feet of mud and even climbed large hills of rocks and boulders with ease.

Charlie complained to Raymond that he couldn't find a job because he had no way to get to and from work. Pleadings from Charlie, eventually convinced Raymond to co-sign for Charlie to purchase a new pick-up truck from a local Chevrolet dealer.

Before signing to guarantee the loan, Raymond pleaded with Charlie to take extreme care of his new vehicle explaining that he couldn't afford to make the payments if Charlie faulted on the loan.

Raymond made it clear that if Charlie neglected his new truck, that he would lose his only transportation to find and keep a job.

Raymond guaranteed the loan with his signature and waved

bye, bye to Charlie as he drove away from the lot in his new shiny-red pick up.

Charlie drove straight to his friends house! Together they were going to break in his new truck at the local wetlands swamp.

With less that ten-miles on the odometer, Charlie shoved the accelerator to the floor and plowed through the woods, flattening trees and shrubs to the ground. Then came the rocks, boulders and finally the mud-bogging.

After more than two hours of leveling an acre of woods, the truck started to over heat and stall.

After digging the pick-up out of the mud, Charlie drove the battered vehicle back to the dealer and parked the mud packed wreck on the new car lot.

The sales person was in total shock to see this new pick-up truck covered in mud with the wheel wells packed solid with shrubs and dirt and numerous dents about the cab. Scraping away some of the mud with his hand the salesperson could see the fresh paint was all scratched and marred.

The sales person looked at Charlie and said; "am I to assume this is the new pick-up that you purchased and drove off this lot about three hours ago?"

Charlie replied; "yeah… and it ain't nothin but a pile of shit and I want my money back!"

Charlie followed with; "It doesn't stand up to your television advertisements, it over-heats and stalls in a little mud!"

The sales person advised Charlie that the new car guarantee wouldn't cover the damages because of intentional abuse and neglect. That all the damage was done in less than three hours and under thirty-miles total driving time!

Charlie said; "I don't give a shit, the truck is yours!" …"I don't want it!"

Charlie and his buddy walked off the lot, leaving the battered vehicle where he had parked it.

Within minutes, Raymond received a telephone call from the dealer requesting that he come to the new car lot.

Upon arriving, both Raymond and Alice almost fainted when they saw what Charlie had done to that new shiny-red pick up truck.

Raymond was advised by the sales department that regardless of what Charlie had done to the truck it was still the property of both Charlie and Raymond and that no repairs would be made concerning the deliberate damages.

Raymond was still responsible for making the monthly payments until the loan was paid in full.

Raymond drove the wreck off the lot and drove it home. The pick up truck remained in Raymond's back yard until he could find a buyer willing to take it off his hands, at a serious loss!

By and by, Charlie found a job driving an eighteen wheeler over the road. He is still a fat-slob, driving for a living and at the truck-stop eateries he is one of the most recognized truckers in America!

In Raymond's case, he could eat as much at one meal as the average man would eat all day. Just looking at Raymond it was obvious that he loved to eat.

His stomach was so big that the lining ruptured and his stomach split open, calling for emergency surgery. The surgery was touch and go because the lining of his stomach was stretched so thin, that stitches wouldn't hold.

The surgeons were forced to close his stomach with metal-clamps.

He developed an infection and remained in Intensive-Care on the critical list for fifteen days.

I remember when the surgeons called all the family together at the hospital and gave us a serious warning to wit:

"If Raymond survives and leaves this hospital alive, it will be a miracle." ..."If he does leave here, he must lose at least one hundred pounds and remain on a very strict diet or he'll die within a year!" ..."If his stomach ever splits open again, there's no way we can close him up." ..."the lining is just too thin and weak!"

Raymond did survive the surgery and was eventually released to go home.

Raymond's wife Alice had a decent office job and with the social security disability check, they managed to survive.

Because they were so tightly strapped financially, Raymond and Alice were limited as to any recreational activity other than to visit mama in Jacksonville every week-end. They lived approximately forty-five miles southeast of Jacksonville in a mobile-home, which mama purchased for them with a second-mortgage on her house.

Every week-end, Raymond and Alice would drive up to mama's house, spending the week-end there. Mama always cooked good meals for Raymond.

Good meals weren't enough though because he would slip away to the Krispy-Kreme Doughnut Shop and come home with a couple dozen hot-glazed-sugar-coated mouth watering doughnuts!

Raymond thought he had to eat them all while they were still warm.

During the week while Alice was at work Raymond's mind would start to work on him. He was depressed about losing his ability to work and bored with watching TV talk and game shows fifteen hours a day, so he took up a hobby.

While watching the cooking shows on television, Raymond decided to take up gourmet cooking as a way to pass the time. He thought it would be nice to reward his wife for her contribution to the family support, by having a delicious hot meal ready and on the table when she came in from work every evening. And that he did!

As a result of Raymond's new hobby, he eventually ate himself to death. Alice found him dead of a massive heart attack, lying across the bed when she came in from work one evening.

At Raymond's funeral, we had to purchase an oversized coffin to hold his remains. In fact, mama paid for the whole funeral since he had no insurance and Alice was financially unable!

Mama, Robert and myself will miss him dearly for as long as we live.

We know that he is in Heaven with our Lord because Raymond accepted Christ as his Savior just weeks before he passed away.

As for Alice, she sold the mobile-home, never offering to share any of the sale with mama who bought it for them in the first place.

Alice put the money in her own pocket and never came around mama again.

We miss you Raymond.

JOHNNY SAVAGE

Thinking back on my childhood in the 1940s, I never heard of or knew anything about illegal drugs. The words "Coke", "Pot", "Snort", "Crack" or "Acid" meant just what it said and had nothing to do with illegal drugs.

Coke was a soft-drink. Pot was something you cooked with. Snort was what you heard from a hog. Crack was in the sidewalk. Acid was to clean parts with.

The big thing for young boys in those days was to sneak off in the woods with our best buddy, smoke a cigarette or cigar, drink a cold can of beer, turn green and vomit!

As children, we never had any money to do anything else so we looked for ways to be creative and have fun. I was two years younger than Raymond and Robert, but a whole lot smarter. Raymond was big in stature, but had little mental maturity. As for Robert, he has always played with less than a full-deck.

Sometimes the finished product of my creativity got me in a lot of trouble. I was always talking Raymond and Robert into something that I knew nothing about.

I could fantasize the outcome in my mind and at the same time, convince my two brothers that I had every detail worked out.

Raymond could literally fly!
When Raymond was ten years old, I convinced him that if he would take mama's new umbrella, climb up on top of our old two-story house and jump off, that he would glide down to the ground safely.

With the umbrella open, I showed him how the underside would catch the air by swinging the umbrella around in a circle.

Raymond swung the umbrella around a time or two and could feel the resistance from the wind. With that, I convinced him that the umbrella would act as a parachute if he would jump off the rooftop and hold the umbrella handle straight up and hold on tight.

Everything appeared to be as I had explained so Raymond climbed to the rooftop and made preparations to jump.

Looking down, Raymond decided to change his mind. I began fast-talking and offered to put mama's old galvanized washtub bottom side up on the ground where he would land.

I explained to Raymond how the bottom of the washtub would act as a cushion in the unlikely event that he came down too fast, that he could land feet-first in the center of the tub and just bounce.

With that ridiculous explanation, Raymond put his trust in me and holding mama's umbrella above his head in the open position, he jumped!

Needless to say, the umbrella turned inside out and Raymond came down off the two-story roof tumbling end over end. He landed sideways across that washtub causing a compound fracture of his left arm and destroying mama's new umbrella.

I started yelling and blaming Raymond for everything. I wanted to know what the hell he was going to do about replacing mama's umbrella and washtub.

Of course, I ran immediately to tell mama that Raymond had just destroyed her new umbrella and wash-tub. I was still blaming everything on him as he was being loaded into an ambulance.

All the explanations and excuses in the world didn't prevent mama from giving me an ass whipping that I still remember to this day!

When Raymond came home from the hospital, he was in a plaster cast from his wrist to his shoulder. I tried to explain to him exactly what he did wrong making his jump, but he just wouldn't listen.

As for committing any criminal acts or violence that never crossed our minds.

Being extremely poor and abused, I did on one occasion allow myself to be talked into doing something that I never quite got over. Still today fifty-five years later, it bothers my conscious.

I was about ten-years old when my good buddy and school mate Parnell Williams asked me to crawl with him on my belly under the old "shotgun" house where he lived. Parnell lived in poverty conditions with his mother, a divorcee. Parnell's father, who had re-married was a detective with the Jacksonville Police Department.

Under the old house, Parnell wanted to show me his secret hiding place where he kept and hid important stuff!

There was no worry about anybody finding his hiding place because only some half-brained idiot would dare crawl under that dark, cold, damp house with all the "Black-Widow" spiders, snakes, rats and roaches to look for anything!

Once under the house, Parnell took a flashlight and showed me his secret hiding place on top of a major floor support beam.

Hidden there, he showed me some extremely valuable collectable antique items that he had stolen from an antique storage warehouse that was located on his early morning paper route.

Parnell told me that he would climb up a drainpipe on the backside of this warehouse where antiques were stored, enter a rear window and loot small, but beautiful things.

The items needed to be small enough to fit into his canvas bag, used to deliver rolled-up newspapers on his bicycle route.

To make sure the information he shared with me would remain top-secret, he convinced me that I was now as much a part of this crime as he was. Knowing that I would never squeal on my buddy, Parnell committed me even more by giving me a beautiful hand carved solid ivory knife and case, hand-made out of a small elephant tusk.

He also gave me a beautiful gold carved jewelry box with a breathtaking inlaid ivory cameo in the lid.

As for the knife, I later learned that this was an actual "Suicide Ceremonial" knife, handed down through generations by Japanese families of great honor and stature. It was obvious even to me, that these were extremely valuable items.

Parnell had a large stash of small but beautiful antique objects to include jewelry, gold hair-combs, music boxes, jewelry boxes, silverware, knives, small swords, an ivory chess-set, carvings and awesome statuettes.

Now just what in the hell was a couple of grammar-school boys living in total poverty going to do with such beautiful and valuable antique collectibles as these?

I did what Parnell did and crawled under my old "shotgun" house and found me a secret hiding place to put my things.

In an effort to drag me in deeper and to assure himself that I would never talk, he took me on his paper route one morning about four o'clock. We climbed up that old drain-pipe, entered the warehouse and made another haul of stolen loot.

I remember there were many beautiful larger items such as oil paintings, dishes, crystal and furniture from around the world that were too large and bulky for us to handle. We could only carry smaller items back down that drain pipe or drop them to the ground.

Parnell and I had quite an attractive pile of loot and no idea what to do with it. We stored the loot for months, before deciding it would be safe to sell some of the smaller items for cash.

I remember that we found what I described as a "scum-bag" looking man, wearing grease stained clothes, working in an old gasoline filling station as we called them back then.

His name was Delbert. We thought it safe to approach him because he looked worse than any criminal I had ever seen in the movies.

I asked Delbert ("the scum-bag"), if he knew anybody that would be interested in buying an old antique knife?

Looking at me strange, I'm sure that Delbert knew the knife was "hot". Even so, he still wanted to know more about it.

Feeling safe now, Parnell and I delivered the knife for Delbert's inspection. Without hesitation, he offered five-dollars for the knife, which we accepted.

Delbert obviously bought a knife that he knew was worth hundreds if not thousands, for five-bucks.

Delbert immediately inquired about any other stuff that we might have for sale. As a way to raise easy quick cash, we sold him a number of other beautiful items for not much more than "peanuts"!

I never knew what Delbert did with this precious loot, but I can only guess that he made a real handsome profit for himself.

As for Parnell and I, we took the five-dollars here and ten-dollars there and blew it all on movies, fast food, candy, yo-yo's and pin-ball machines!

Looking back now, I sold all the stuff that I hid under my house. Parnell on the other hand, moved away with his mother to South Carolina, leaving behind all that valuable loot still in his secret hiding place under that old house. Only God knows whatever happened to all that valuable loot.

I can only imagine that the old "shotgun" house has long since been torn down and some poor demolition worker is now comfortably retired and living off the wealth of his discovery. If the house is still standing, I guess the loot is still there covered in cobwebs and rat shit!

Just for fun, I was able to contact my old buddy Parnell by computer a few months ago. I hadn't talked with him in more than fifty years.

When I reminded him about this incident in our past, he replied: "Oh dear God, don't ever bring that up again, I am a Christian man, who would like to erase that memory from my past!"

We both laughed, but we have enough sense to know that what we did was very wrong.

We couldn't help but wonder, what ever did happen to all that priceless loot hidden under that old "shotgun" house?

Just out of curiosity, I think I'll drive by that old house the next time I'm in the Jacksonville area, just to see if it still stands. If it does, I guarantee the loot is still there in Parnell's old secret hiding place!

Giving up crime at age eleven, I got me a job at Saver's Super Market on Forrest Street, a few blocks from our house. I was too young to expect anything more than my wage of sixty-cents an hour, sacking groceries at the checkout counter.

My boss, Irving Goldstein was the storeowner who took a liking to me right away. He always wanted me to sack groceries at his counter because I was fast, did what I was told and minded my own business.

Irving was one shrewd operator, who knew how to make money.

He could run his fingers across the keys of a cash register so fast, that it was impossible to follow his ringing with your eyes.

He would up the price a few cents on several items with every customer that went through his checkout counter. Because he was so fast, almost nobody ever caught him stealing.

In those days there was no such thing as an electronic-scanner like we see in our present day super-markets.

The cashiers would punch in every item by hand and they were super fast with no concern about over-pricing an item every eight or ten rings.

Irving had a super scam going and he ran this particular scam all day, every day on his check out counter. Here is how it worked:

When I would arrive for work after school every afternoon,

Irving would send me to the broom section of the store and order me to bring back a large household sweeping-broom.

Irving would take this broom, stand it up beside the checkout counter where the buggies were unloaded and then he would deliberately charge every customer that came through his checkout a dollar-eighty-five cents for that broom.

Because he was so fast with his fingers, he was rarely challenged for ringing those dollar-eighty-five cents. On rare occasions a customer would say: "hold it, wait a minute... you charged me for something that I didn't have in my shopping cart!"

Irving would stop ringing and pull the register detail tape up, as though looking for some error. He would start calling off the last eight or ten items that he rang until he got to the broom.

The customer would say: "I didn't buy no damn broom!"

With that comment Irving would say; "this isn't your broom?" Then he would apologize for ringing the broom, explaining that the broom was standing there against the counter and he thought the customer had brought it to the checkout!

The customers never noticed or questioned the broom leaning against the counter because they just thought it was part of the stores cleaning supplies.

Irving would then turn toward me and with a quick wink, he would shout; "see what you've done boy?" "You've caused me to charge this customer for something they didn't want!"

Then he would follow with; "now take your broom to the backroom where it belongs, so this doesn't happen again!" "Apologize to this customer before you go!"

I'd apologize to the customer, while Irving would deduct the illegal charge.

I'd take the new broom to the back of the store like Irving said. By the time I returned to the checkout counter the irate customer had left, and he'd say; "boy, get your ass to the back and bring me my broom!"

Irving would once again stand the broom up against the counter and charge the next unsuspecting customer for that same broom all over again!

We must have sold that same broom a thousand times while I worked there.

At the end of each shift, Irving would always give me a day old Angel-Food Cake as a reward for keeping quiet about his broom-scam. I don't know why it was always Angel-Food Cake, but it was. I couldn't stand the taste of Angel-Food Cake!

By the time I reached thirteen, I had self-taught myself a great deal about two-cycle and four-cycle small engines. Being too poor to have a professional mechanic work on my old motor scooters and junk cycles, I'd make my own repairs to include tearing down and re-building the engines.

At fifteen, I got me a grease-monkey job at Rick's BSA Motorcycle Shop on Kings Avenue in Jacksonville, Florida. I worked there in a position called a "koolie" until I was sixteen. A koolie was the low man on the totem pole, who washed grease from the cycles before the mechanics worked on them. A koolie also would tear down engines so the mechanics could then re-build them.

I was also called a "gofer", meaning go-for-this and go-for-that!

I had so much fun and was proud to be part of the shop team.

I was so skinny back then that the guys I worked with would tease me and say; "you're skinny enough to use a Kotex-wrapper as a sleeping-bag!" Because I was so skinny and light, I was allowed to race the shop dragster bike. Being so light, it was like the dragster was running down the drag strip all by itself.

I later ranked as expert and made a strong name for myself on the race circuit to include flat-track oval racing.

Later on in life after serving four years in the U.S. Air Force, I finally made the "Big-One" at the Daytona International Speedway, where I set sixteen national and international records in the 250cc class.

Approaching age seventeen and very unhappy, I ran away from home and got me a job as a motorcycle ("koolie") mechanic with the James E. Strait Fair, a traveling carnival show. I worked for an awesome motorcycle act, keeping the cycles in good safe running order.

Back then, a family consisting of a father Jack and two sons would ride motorcycles around the inside walls of a wooden circular dome. They were crazier than they were skilled!

They would ride these motorcycles up on the walls of this large wooden bowl dome that stood about forty-feet tall.

If you can imagine using your finger to spin a marble inside a coffee cup and watching that marble spin around the inside walls of the cup, then you can somewhat visualize the thrill of this act.

While riding, they would sit on the motorcycles side-ways, backwards, blindfolded, standing-up and even criss-cross each other on the wall with two motorcycles traveling in different directions.

The riders would ride up the walls within inches of the paid spectators. This was one exciting show to watch and extremely scary, when the riders would come within inches of the spectator's heads as they looked down inside this forty-foot tall wooden bowl.

The roar of the open exhaust pipes, the smell of the exhaust and screeching rubber tires would cause some women to back away and sometimes faint!

This family of three was nothing short of full-blown alcoholics, who lived in a motor home while traveling with the carnival show from state to state.

I guess they had to stay drunk; to ride these walls five or six times a night. As I remember, they spent all day sitting around their motor home drinking whiskey and fighting prior to gate opening each night. Then it was back on the walls again!

About a week after I went to work for them, Jack came over one morning to the dome where I was adjusting the cycles chains and sprockets.

I told him that his motorcycle act was the most thrilling thing I had ever seen before in my life. I told him about my riding and racing experience, but nothing to me seemed more exciting than this act!

Prior to the actual shows, this family of three would ride motorcycles on the front-platform of the dome on steel rollers mounted to the stage under the front and rear wheels of the cycles. They did this to excite the carnival crowd, to entice them into buying a ticket to come inside and watch them ride on the walls.

The cycle on the platform was actually secured to the stage floor by a heavy-duty steel chain. If that cycle ever came off the rollers or if the rider ever fell, the motorcycle would have traveled off the stage and into the crowd of spectators. Without a doubt, somebody would have been killed!

I remember one night, a son in the act was so drunk that he couldn't perform. Jack asked me if I wanted to ride the rollers on the front platform and thrill the spectators. I'd been waiting for this opportunity and within minutes, I was on the rollers and riding like a true professional. I stood up, rode side-ways, backwards, blindfolded and experienced a real rush like nothing I had known before.

The next morning, Jack came over to the dome again and asked me if I wanted to ride the walls. There was no hesitation on my part because I knew that I would probably never have this opportunity to ride the walls again.

I remember Jack instructing me to start a slow climb around the slanted base of the wall until I could get up enough speed to shift into second gear. Once in second gear, I was to twist full-throttle and climb up onto the bottom section of the wall.

Then over the roar of the engine, looking up at me and standing in the bottom of that giant wooden-bowl, he started to scream out instructions.

"The centrifugal force will keep you up there boy."

"Always look forward at the white line in the center of the dome, just like riding down the highway!"

"Don't look down until I tell you it's okay… do you understand?"

"I understand!" shouting back!

After a minute or so, I had gained enough speed and centrifugal force to reach the center of the wall, was scared shitless, but stable.

"Keep looking straight ahead at the white line and imagine that you're running down the interstate at fifty miles per hour!"

Shouting back again, I just said: "okay!"

Looking straight ahead, it was like running down the centerline of the interstate with nothing ahead of me except highway. In reality, I knew dammed well that I was up on a wooden wall, inside a large forty-foot bowl, running fifty miles per hour.

"Let go of the handle-bars and hold your arms straight up", shouted Jack.

I did what he said and felt no difference than riding hands free down an open highway.

One trick after another, until I was riding the wall as well as I had handled the steel rollers on the platform.

Jack then shouted: "do you see the bright-red stripe at the top of the wall?" ... "Slowly steer your way up there, but under no circumstances do you ever want to cross that red line." ... "do you understand?"

I eased up to the bright-red line and ran the front wheel of the motorcycle within inches of the line.

"If you cross that bright-red line, you're dead!" ... he shouted!

He was referring to the fact that inches beyond that bright-red line was the spectator's heads, looking down inside the dome.

The only thing that separated the spectator from the motorcycle and rider was a steel strand of cable that ran around the top inside lip of the wall. This was to keep the motorcycle from accidentally slipping up and over the wall into the spectator's faces.

To hit that steel safety-cable would mean sure disaster for the rider!

"Coming down is no problem!" he shouted.

"Start backing off the throttle and you lose speed!" ... "The loss of speed will eliminate the centrifugal force that's holding you up there!"

I did what he said and came safely down to the bottom of the dome. I had to really get on the brakes to stop within the few feet of space at the bottom. Otherwise, I would hit the wall head on!

I was then allowed to ride the "Wall Of Death" as they billed it in a number of shows.

Jack had nothing to lose and everything to gain by having a young good-looking kid riding the " Wall Of Death" on a minimum wage.

I was having so much fun that I honestly believe I would have paid Jack to let me ride the walls.

All good things must end because my father had tracked me down to the carnival stop over in Tampa, Florida.

I was riding the wall in all my glory, when I spotted my father looking down inside the dome at my antics.

As soon as the act was over, old Sylvester took me by my collar and lead me away from that carnival and my short-lived days of glory!

Things weren't so merry around our house when I got home, so I finished my senior year of high-school at Jacksonville Technical School and made a decision that I knew would ease the burdens on the household expenses and would be a blessing to Sylvester.

Following in the footsteps of my older brothers, I joined the military directly out of high school in an effort to get myself as far away as I could from the miserable home life that I was living in.

WINDFALL TO HEARTBREAK

As a fifteen year old boy, I was ready to graduate from my old Cushman Motor Scooter to a dream that had become an obsession.

My every thought was to own a beautiful custom built "Chopper" motorcycle, covered in chrome, custom painted, with my own custom designed exhaust system!

With virtually no chance of finding the financial means to do this, I decided to build this obsession piece by piece. If I could afford only one small part each payday, then it was at least a start. Regardless of how long it would take to complete my project, I was committed to do just that.

At great sacrifice to include skipping some meals to pay for needed parts, I kept my project going. Virtually all the meager cash in my pay envelopes went toward another needed part.

Week after week, month after month, I assembled part by part until I could see my chopper begin to take shape.

First came the frame, then the wheels, forks, handlebars and fenders. I really got excited at this point because I could for the first time in ten months see the outline of my obsession standing there upright and looking good!

This only made me work harder with such enthusiasm that my friends accused me of foaming at the mouth on occasion.

The engine was my greatest obstacle, due to the tremendous cost in bringing a stock basic scratch engine to a complete modified racing powerhouse.

I chose Milton Ricks of Rick's BSA Cycles in Jacksonville, Florida to rebuild my engine. Rick's reputation for building screaming machines was well known in the cycle circles.

Although a fifteen year age difference separated us, Rick and I became friends for life.

I worked at his shop after school and every weekend for a full year to pay off the cost of my engine. I needed the engine mounted so I could decide on one of several ideas for the gas tank that must not only fit properly, but mold into the flow-lines of the other pieces already in place.

The seat and upholstery materials had to make a statement, flowing from the same lines and shape of the gas tank.

The exhaust pipes were modified from a set of original exhausts off a 1940s Indian Chief Motorcycle. Once cut, welded and chrome plated, the two exhaust pipes resembled a Cobra Snake in a strike position. I actually named them "Cobra Pipes!"

The custom wiring and running lights completed my chopper. From here the chopper had to be completely dismantled for custom paint and chrome plating.

Everything that could be chrome plated was. The frame was painted metallic black to enhance the shiny chrome plated engine cases and other accessories.

The fenders, gas and oil tanks were painted metallic purple and pin striped in gold. Once reassembled, my chopper was nothing short of a masterpiece.

It was an emotional moment of pure joy when I started the engine for the first time. I will never, ever forget that unique sound produced from this awesome powerhouse and then coming forth from my Cobra Pipes!

No written words could ever describe the beauty and power of my new chopper. Just know, that it rode like a dream, was a true work of art and was all mine!

Because it was fast as lightning, I called it "Thunderbolt!"

I rode my chopper only a few months, before I began to serve my time in the Air Force at age seventeen. Before leaving, I took my low mileage chopper over to my grandmother's house and got permission to store it in her garage.

I chose my grandmother to safe keep my chopper because her garage was rarely used and I knew it would be safe there away from theft or my brothers.

I carefully drained the gasoline from the tank, placed the chopper on blocks to keep the tires off the ground and safe from any elements that could cause drying or tire decay. I then covered it with a clean soft blanket and carefully secured the blanket with rope wrapped three times around.

My grandmother assured me that when I returned on my first military leave, my chopper would be there, safe and ready for me to pick up!

Military obligations prevented me from picking up my chopper for several months. During that time, I sent for and married Diane, my high school sweetheart.

I was assigned to the 3320th Air Police Squadron at Amarillo Air Force Base, Texas.

In the 1950s military pay was minimal and living conditions were rough on a young married couple. Diane and I managed to survive, as long as we were content to do without some things that weren't of absolute necessity.

Mama would call us on occasion to see how we were doing financially. She worried about us, so every once in a while her letter would contain a ten or twenty dollar money order. She would advise us to use it for groceries or a utility bill.

I was in the service for about six months before I could arrange leave time to pick up my chopper in Florida and return to Amarillo.

As I was making the leave arrangements, I received a letter

from mama with a money order for seven hundred dollars. You can imagine the shock and awe that both Diane and I experienced when we saw this seven hundred dollar windfall!

Knowing that my mother had limited financial means, I immediately called to thank her for the gift and to ask how she was able to acquire this kind of money. It was just too much for me to comprehend such a gift from mama.

In her calm and sympathetic voice, mama expressed her concern for our financial well-being. She went on to explain that she knew how hard it was for Diane and I to make ends meet on my meager military salary.

Then came mama's explanation of how she was able to accumulate the seven hundred dollars she sent us. Her explanation was a blow that devastated my life until this very day.

Mama very softly said: "Johnny, I worry so much about you and Diane. I know that your survival and comfort at this time is more important than material things!"

"I sold your motorcycle to a sailor stationed at the Jacksonville Naval Air Station for seven hundred dollars!" "He picked it up from your grandmother's house and was very happy with the price!"

"You can always buy another motorcycle after you finish your military tour!"

Dear God, I don't remember if I screamed or fainted, or both! I was absolutely shocked and stunned to a point of losing my voice. My jaw and lips quivered uncontrollably. My heart was crushed!

When I could finally speak, I screamed over and over; "Oh dear God, please God no, no!

Diane not knowing what was going on was also screaming in the background; "what is it, who died, who died?"

I cried out to mama asking how she could do this to me? I told her that the chopper was worth five times what she sold it for, not counting the two years of labor and sacrifice that I endured to build it.

Mama said she was sorry if she made a mistake and then said: "you'll get over it, because time heals everything!"

It's been almost fifty years and I never have gotten over it and I never will.

This incident destroyed my trust in mankind.

After returning from the military, my cycle buddies used me for a while as their personal laughing stock. They consistently asked me how I was able to keep from murdering my mama for what she did!

I did eventually buy me another motorcycle, but knew there would never be another Thunderbolt!

A year or two later, a friend told me that the sailor who bought my chopper had been drag racing and had blown away everything in it's class from Florida to California.

I never did see my chopper again, but I'll bet that lucky sailor enjoyed my work of art for a long, long time!

Military was a break from the Savage Clan:
I wasn't quite eighteen when I joined the Air Force Military Police and was stationed in Amarillo, Texas from 1955 to 1959.

Shortly after my enlistment, I married Diane, my high school sweetheart and started a family of my own. I swore that I'd never allow any of the horrors, grief and misery that haunted the Savage clan to ever find a way into my life again.

I came out of the military with an Honorable Discharge and two beautiful children; Julie and Bruce. Within three years, we were blessed with two more beautiful children; Donna and Jamie.

Diane and I grew up with our children. We were an average type family with much love for and from our children with never a trace of the suffering and grief that I had experienced in my childhood.

Because Diane and I were only children ourselves when we married and started our own family, we missed all the normal fun things that other teens experience.

We were completely devoted to raising our children and just trying to financially survive in those days!

As a result, twenty-eight years into our marriage with the children grown and on their own, Diane and I grew apart and had an amicable divorce. Twenty-years later, we remain friends!

Years later I married Debbie, who slept with my best friend while I was out of town working.

Needless to say, I set a new world-record in obtaining a divorce. I gave her half the pots and pans and sent her ass on up the highway!

In my fifty's and swearing that I would never marry again, I met and married a precious Christian lady named Joanie, who had three grown children of her own.

We are a Christian yoked couple, happily married for ten-years at this writing. Between us, we have seven children, thirteen grandchildren and three great grandchildren.

My three daughters live in Atlanta, Georgia and my only son lives in Jacksonville, Florida.

RACISM and IGNORANCE

As a child in the 1940s, I grew up in great fear of and with absolutely no respect what-so-ever for any black person.

Black and white alike have been indoctrinated by a myth of fear and distrust for more than a hundred-years. When I was a child, that distrust was at it's peak.

Back then, the only descriptive comment referring to a black person that I ever heard on a daily basis was; "Nigger!"

Other words commonly used by my peers were; "Jigaboo", "Coon", "Spade", "Negroid" and "Spook".

The blacks lived in their own isolated community that white's referred to as; "Nigger Town!"

Segregation is not a good word to describe the separation between the blacks and whites in those days. There was an imaginary line that separated the blacks from the whites, like the "Mason/Dixon Line" or the "50th Parallel" during war time.

That line was at the very top of a hill on May Street. Once you topped that hill, you were either in nigger-town or you were entering the area of poor white-trash, depending on which way you were traveling.

Either way, your travels were extremely dangerous, depending on the color of your skin! If you chose to cross that line, you either had a death wish or you were one tough son-of-a-bitch!

I was afraid of all black people and was taught to stay as far away from them as possible.

No matter how hard I tried to keep my distance, they were impossible to avoid.

Sooner or later, I would find myself confronted by some black kid my age and without reason, we would go to war.

The black kids knew how the white kids felt about them, so we were always ready for a fight.

Fights would break out for no reason what-so-ever, just because by accident, we came across each other.

Some of my most brutal fights as a youth were with nameless black kids my age, that I had never met before and didn't even know why we were fighting.

I grew up being taught that all black people possessed severely under developed brains and were dangerous. I was taught by my peers, that they were descendents from the ape species, who roamed the streets at night looking for trouble or anything they could steal. In general, I thought they lived and ate like animals!

Sylvester used to tell me and my brothers, that niggers loved to riot. Not for some political, social or domestic reason, but because they wanted some new clothes, furniture, appliance or something.

He said a nigger would riot at the drop of a hat, so they could break out storefront windows and run down the streets with armloads of stolen merchandise, running by helpless police officers, laughing and screaming like a bunch of hyenas, as they headed home with their stolen loot!

Sylvester would tell us that during their riots, the niggers would burn down their own businesses and homes. They would riot again a few months later, if the Federal Government balked at rebuilding their community with the working white man's tax money!

I remember Sylvester saying that a nigger was born to steal.

That they had a bred instinct in their genes that made them steal. That they couldn't control the urge to steal, if the opportunity was there.

Sylvester would tell me a story, where he said that scientists had proven without a doubt, that a nigger couldn't control the urge to steal.

He said that a team of scientists took a three-year old white boy, sat him on the floor, spread his legs and rolled a new brightly-colored rubber ball to him.

That, the white child would look and touch the beautiful ball and then by coaxing, would roll the ball back to the scientist, like a game of catch!

Then came the three-year old black boy's turn, where the same ball was rolled to him. The black boy would look and touch the pretty ball and then take it and roll it behind his back, in an attempt to hide it.

When the scientist tried to coax the black boy to roll the ball back, he kept the ball hidden behind his back, looking at the scientist as though there never was any ball.

Thus, as Sylvester said; "this proves without a doubt, that even a three-year old nigger can't resist the urge to steal!"

"Again, proving that the urge to steal is inbred in all niggers!"

Old Sylvester also had it in for the Jews, who he despised. He claimed that the reason Jews had all the money, was because they never trusted anyone in the human race, not even their own kind.

Jews he said, were driven by greed, they were cheap and they hoarded all the wealth, not just in America, but all over the world!

Sylvester said that's why they chose names like Goldstein and Silverstein, because they owned all the gold and silver!

Sylvester would tell the story of how the Jewish men would teach their children at a very early age, to never, ever trust anyone, not even their own parents.

Sylvester would tell it this way: When a Jewish child reached the age of two and could stand upright on their own, it was the fathers job to take the child into the kitchen and stand the child on the edge of the kitchen table.

The Jewish father would then start clapping his hands and saying to the child; "come on baby, jump into daddy's arms!"... "Daddy will catch you!" "It's OK, baby, jump to daddy!"

After a few minutes of coaxing and pleading, the baby would leap forward to daddy's outstretch arms. At this point, the father would step back and let the baby crash to the floor, smashing it's face on the hard tile!

The Jewish father would then pick up the crying child, wipe the blood from it's little mouth and nose and then scream into the baby's face; "this will teach you never to trust anyone in this world."

"Don't ever trust any son-of-a-bitch,... not even your own parents!"

I will never forget when Sylvester first told me that Jews don't believe in Jesus! Now I couldn't imagine that there were people in this world that didn't believe in Jesus, so I went looking for a Jew to ask!

I was about six years old, when I walked down to the corner of the block where I lived to confront the owner of a small store called Jack's Grocery.

I knew that Jack was a Jew, because I remember Sylvester always cursing and complaining that Jack charged double the prices for the same items that the A&P Supermarket charged.

I also remember Sylvester saying that you could always spot a Jew, because their last name always ended in a lot of S's, Z's, Q's, Y's, W's and X's!

In innocent ignorance, I walked right up to Jack Markowitz and said: "Jack, my father said that you don't believe in Jesus,... is that true?"

Old Jack looked at me in shock and replied; "I do believe there was a Rabbi named Jesus, who was a great teacher, who did some wonderful things,... but, I don't believe he was the Messiah!"

I had no idea what Rabbi or the Messiah meant, but I did hear Jack say that he believed in the man named Jesus, so I went back home and told my father that he was wrong!

Needless to say, I got my ass whipped for repeating to Jack what my father had said. I never did understand why, but I learned not to repeat much of what my father had to say in anger, after that.

Well anyway, getting back to the niggers, we had separate schools, play-grounds, rest rooms, water fountains, restaurants and theaters. Blacks were forced to sit in the last three rows of the public-city-bus and had to stand up and give whitey their seat, if the bus became over crowded.

As a child, I was totally ignorant concerning blacks or their feelings.

I lived like I was taught by my peers, to fear and despise all blacks.

I remember that blacks were placed in one of two categories. There was the regular, everyday "Local Nigger," then there was the "Sand-Nigger!"

A sand-nigger was anyone with black skin that came from the desert countries, such as; India, Iraq, Iran, Egypt, Arabia, etc.

I was taught that the sand nigger was also dangerous, but was a better class of nigger, because their skin was black from the sun and the extreme heat of the desert. That their skin was in fact half-cooked !

The good old USA Southern Nigger was mostly animal, imported from the jungles of Africa, as replacements for mules, to plow land for the cotton farmers.

None of this bothered me during my youth, because this was just a way of life and was an imbedded part of my upbringing. To put it bluntly, I didn't know anything else to describe a black person, other than to call them "Nigger."

I want to tell you, the impact this had on me and recount a time when I came to realize, that black people were not the animals that were described to me by my peers.

I was seventeen years of age, when I joined the United States

Air Force in 1955. I was sent to Lackland Air Force Base for my basic-training.

You can imagine the shock, when I found a good number of blacks in my squadron, who were actually going to sleep in the same barracks with me, eat at the same table, bathe in the same shower and drink from the same water fountains. I couldn't believe my eyes, but I knew better than to express my concern!

In training side by side with the blacks, each day got a little easier, as conversations were starting to develop between some of the blacks and myself.

I soon realized that they could hold a conversation and didn't live or eat like animals, as I was previously taught. As a matter of fact, I started to develop a real friendship with one black named; Alvin Price.

The basic training was brutal, and it was a good warm feeling to have a buddy to help me get through each day. Alvin and I started to team up when our training required two basic-trainees to complete a task. After a while, Alvin and I just became partners, helping each other survive.

After basic-training, we were both transferred and assigned to the 3320th Air Police Squadron at Amarillo Air Force Base, Amarillo, Texas.

After our ten-week military police training, we were assigned our regular military police duties and were also assigned as a team to the emergency rescue/security unit, in the event of an aircraft crash or disaster situation.

Everything at the base rocked along well between Alvin and I, where we both were always trying to out do each other. If Alvin did something outstanding and got recognition, then I had to do something better. We were always in competition, trying to outshine each other, which became amusing to our commanding officers.

Even so, we respected each other and would always recognize the accomplishments of the other. There was never an ounce of envy or resentment between either of us.

One hot summer afternoon, Alvin and I were dispatched to a remote desert location, where a classified Air Force Fighter Jet had gone down.

Driving for hours in the desert, Alvin and I arrived at the scene and took control of the crash site from the local police. We set up flood lights, roped off the site and secured the area, pending the crash scene investigators arrival.

I remember that the two of us remained there for about a week, until the investigators finished their task, and the aircraft remains were trucked away.

Both Alvin and I were tired of eating the dry canned K-Rations that were packed in our emergency vehicle and thought of nothing more than a real home cooked, hot, tasty meal.

Driving away from the crash site, we started looking along the highway for the first appealing restaurant to surface. About half way back to the base, we came upon a restaurant in Borger, Texas, where a big road-sign read; "Country-Kitchen Hot Meals."

I turned our truck into the gravel drive and parked. We ran to the front door and once inside, we grabbed a booth and were ready to eat. All that Alvin and I could think about was plenty of fried chicken, mashed potatoes, beans and hot cornbread.

The restaurant was about three-quarters full of white customers, most were already eating. We got a lot of stares and no service, which I couldn't understand, since we were both in military fatigues and wearing our military-police insignias.

After waiting for about fifteen-minutes, the waitress who was openly embarrassed, said: "I want you to know, this isn't my feelings, but I was instructed by the owner to tell you that we don't serve niggers in our dining room!"

She then said, pointing at me; "we will serve you in the dining room, but your friend will have to eat his dinner in the kitchen!"

I was in total shock, as her words tore at my heart. I was both angry and extremely embarrassed for my friend Alvin.

How in God's name, could these people be so ignorant as to make such a statement. To deny a good and honorable military man the right to pay for and eat a meal, just because of his skin-color?

I got all choked up when Alvin said; "It's ok John, you go ahead and eat, and I'll wait for you in the truck!"

I got up and walked out the door with Alvin, as the waitress said; "I'm so sorry, it wasn't my decision!"

The drive back to the base was very quiet, with a lot of hurt and very little conversation between Alvin and myself.

I was without words in my shock, when I came to realized that the reaction of those people back at that restaurant, their bigotry, and racist attitude, was more or less that of a former southern-born racist, who was presently driving the truck

I looked at myself in the rear view mirror and thought back a few years earlier, when I, in my ignorant upbringing, thought just like those ignorant bastards back at the restaurant!

Time heals all things, but I'll never forget that most embarrassing moment in my life, when I was shocked into reality, that God created and loves all of his children the same. That color is only skin-deep and doesn't make up the character of a man.

I haven't seen Alvin since our military days of the 1950s, but we have talked on the telephone a couple of times. Alvin is a college art-professor, living up north. We still have that close bond and respect for each other, and we will always be brothers in our hearts.

God Bless you Alvin, and your family.

GOD SENT AN ANGEL TO TEST ME

I had serious reservations about inserting this segment into my book, because most non believers would scoff it off as nonsense and doubt my sanity.

In my life, I've had two incidents that I refer to as Divine Encounters.

The first one when I was six years old, was shared with you earlier.

I still don't understand the reason for that first Angelic visit, but the second visit left no doubt in my mind what-so-ever.

I am positive that my second encounter was an Angel sent by God to test me. It occurred in December 1990.

I was returning from a business trip from Atlanta to my home in Wildwood, Florida. I remember it was a very cold, rainy evening and I was tired, sleepy and hungry. I pulled off the I-75 exit in Wildwood, and parked at an all night diner.

Entering the eatery, I noticed that only a few tables were occupied at that time of night. The waitress showed me to a booth and handed me the menu.

I noticed sitting across from my booth, was a poorly dressed vagrant who was obviously hungry, wet and cold.

I couldn't help but notice that the vagrant was eating a few Saltine Crackers, and was peeling the paper tops off the small coffee creamers and drinking the contents.

When my waitress returned to take my order, I asked her what the story was concerning the vagrant.

The waitress replied that he was a homeless person, like a lot of others that hung around the truck-stop begging for handouts. She said that he was different than most though, because he only asked for snacks or scraps of food and never money!

The waitress went on to explain that her boss wouldn't allow the employees to feed the homeless, because if they fed just one, then all the others in the area would come seeking the same handouts!

The waitress said that she felt so sorry for this man, emphasizing again, that he only wanted something to eat and never begged for money.

"I can't afford to feed him!"… said the waitress,… "but I just had to give him a few crackers and a few extra creamers!"

With that, I told the waitress to give the vagrant a menu and to tell him that he could order anything he wanted, to include hot-coffee and dessert and that I would take care of the check!

I remember as though it were yesterday, that vagrant ate a full course hot meal and topped it off with apple-pie.

He finished his meal before I did, then stood up and walked out of the diner.

The waitress came to my table with the vagrant's check and asked me if he thanked me for the meal, before he walked out!

I replied to the waitress, that it wasn't necessary for him to thank me, that I was just happy, that God had provided me the financial means to help that poor soul.

The waitress got upset and said; "I can't believe that he ate all that food you paid for, and walked out of the restaurant without one word of thanks for what you did!"

The waitress was still boiling mad, when I told her it was okay and not to worry about it!

I was only a few bites from finishing my meal, when I looked up at the large plate glass window facing my booth. Standing there on the sidewalk in the rain and cold, was the vagrant, looking straight at me.

He was standing in the center of the window, with both arms outstretch, looking like a cross, staring straight into my eyes. He had a big bright smile on his face.

With his outstretch arms, he appeared a giant of a man. He then gave me both thumbs up and walked away into the night.

Cold shivers and goose-pimples surfaced all over my body. Without question, God somehow let me know that I had just fed one of his cold, hungry Angels, who was sent for no other reason, than to test me!

This was without question a Divine encounter that I can only explain as a powerful experience that I'll never forget as long as I live.

Even today, twelve years later, I get a shivering feeling when I drive through that area and glance over at that building.

Thank you God for allowing me to be your vessel on that cold, rainy night, to fulfill a prophesy and warnings by Scripture, that these things would come to pass.

I know this to be true, because I am a living witness!

BETTY SAVAGE

"A pitiful wasted life"

Betty was my only sister. Her life was simple, tragic and wasted.

The only mark that Betty left on this earth was three nice children, a disappointed husband and a few sad memories.

Betty was born into this world with poor eye-sight, which was never corrected. Not that attempts weren't made to correct her eye-sight, but lack of knowledge by doctors in the 1930s failed to correct her problem. If anything they made her sight worse.

Betty grew up with a big-chip on her shoulder because of her disability! She was the world's greatest case of self-pity, and she would let anybody and everybody know about it!

As much as our family dreaded the thought of Betty spending her life with poor eye-sight, there was absolutely nothing we could do about it.

We all suffered the consequences of Betty's self-pity and anger. She was always ready to verbally attack anyone who disagreed with her or crossed her in any way.

I remember once when Betty said to mama; "I have a problem with my feet, they hurt me most of the time!"

Mama replied; "most of the Savage children do have bad feet

because of the shoes you were forced to wear while growing up!"

Because mama spoke in general about the feet of all the children, instead of specifically about Betty's problem, all hell broke loose and Betty verbally attacked mama for not having more compassion about her particular problem!

She was as sweet as could be, if you would sit there and listen to her problems, pity her, humor her and agree with everything she had to say.

We all knew that to feed her selfish ego, was a sure way to keep peace and harmony while in her presence.

Betty's husband Warren took the brunt of her abuses, because he was always readily available for her to attack. If Warren wasn't working, he was at home catching pure hell.

Betty would become so enraged at times, she would attack Warren, scratching his face with her finger-nails or slapping the shit out of him. Warren was a gentleman, but had to be on guard twenty-four hours a day to prevent serious injury. His greatest fear was being attacked while he was sleeping.

I remember once when Betty flared up about something while we were watching a TV-program. She started cursing Warren for every son-of-a-bitch that ever lived, so he got up to walk into the kitchen.

When Warren walked past Betty, she jumped up and dug a lit cigarette into his neck, causing a serious burn and blistering of his skin.

This was a typical attack that she would inflict on anybody in her way, when she exploded.

Betty would reach a state of depression and lock herself in her bedroom for days on end. Never once coming out to even eat. She would just sit in there smoking cigarettes and drinking warm beer that she stored under her bed by the case.

Betty hated her brother Harold, because she was absolutely convinced that he cheated her and the other family members out of a portion of Sylvester's estate when he died.

As mentioned earlier in this story, the entire family suspected that Harold found Sylvester's stashed loot after his death and kept it for himself.

There was also the incident where Harold looted our grandmother's house at her death, and stripped the house of all the antiques for his own selfish greed. Betty never forgot about this either!

Betty was also furious at mama for allowing Harold to take everything for himself and not sharing with the other brothers and herself.

After Sylvester's death, Betty actually retained a lawyer and filed a civil-suit against mama for her fair share of Sylvester's estate.

By the time the lawyers got their third of Betty's share, she received only a few hundred dollars, because Sylvester's suspected stashed loot was never found, *according to Harold*!!??

Betty separated herself from all the family including mama after filing the law-suit, and for more than twelve years, never spoke to or laid eyes on any member of the Savage clan, until the day before she died.

Betty was in a Georgia hospital, on her death bed when mama called me on the phone and said; "Johnny, your sister is dying, and I don't intend to let her die without talking to me one last time!"

"She's my only daughter, I love her and I want to tell her that, before she dies!"

"I don't care if she doesn't want to see me, I'm going to her anyway!"

"Will you please come and take me to see her?"

I told mama to pack an overnight bag, that I'd leave immediately and pick her up.

Raymond and Robert were there when I arrived and the four of us drove to south Georgia to see my sister.

We arrived in time for each of us to visit with her for a few minutes, before she died. Betty recognized all of us and had a soft touching talk with mama. Betty died a few hours later.

Grief, misery, suffering and self-pity was all she ever knew. Betty is gone, but not forgotten.

ON THE LIGHTER SIDE

Warren, my brother-in-law, tried to take up the slack where my father failed. In other words, he did things for Raymond, Robert and myself, that my father never accepted as his responsibility.

Warren would on occasion take us fishing, to a baseball game or to the stock-car races. Without Warren, we would never have seen or experienced many of these things.

Warren played first base for a fast-pitch softball team and he was really sharp. He always took me and my brothers to his games, just so we could get out and have some fun.

I was Warren's favorite, and he would on occasion take me someplace special if the opportunity was right.

I loved going fishing with him and later after a deep-fry process, eating the fish we caught.

I remember that I spent as much time as possible at Warren and Betty's house. Anything or anywhere beat the hell out of listening to the cursing and shouting between Sylvester and mama at our house.

I was spending the day and night with Betty and Warren once, when I witnessed a sight I'll never forget.

There was a man who lived about two blocks away from Warren's house, on the same street. He was a race car driver at the local speedway on Friday nights and drove on the streets in the same reckless manner that he drove on the clay ovals.

Every afternoon about 5:30 P.M., "Mr. Show-Off" race-car driver on his way home from work, would pass Warren's house in his souped-up Chevrolet doing about eighty miles per hour.

You could hear the engine screaming and the gears speed-shifting as he was approaching the direction of Warren's house.

There were many children living and playing near or on the street where Warren and Betty lived, to include three of their own.

Warren had spoken to that race car driver on a number of occasions about his reckless endangerment of the children in the neighborhood, to no avail.

Warren and Corky his next door neighbor, who also had children, decided to put a stop to the hot-rod antics of that race car driver, and came up with this plan:

They would bring home a heavy log called a "Cross-Tie" from the railroad yards. A cross-tie is used as a foundation for laying and securing steel railroad tracks. They are pressure treated to prevent rot and wear and weigh well-over two hundred pounds each.

Warren and Corky would drive a large steel eye-bolt into one end of the cross-tie and secure a nylon rope to the eyelet. They would lay the cross-tie in the woods across the street from Warren's house and then stretch the rope across the street, running it along the side of the house, to the rear where Warren and Corky were holding the opposite end of the rope.

Now here was the plan: When the race car driver was approaching, we would hear him winding up his engine and speed-shifting a block or so before reaching Warren's house.

When he was within one-hundred feet of Warren's house, both Warren and Corky would start running with the nylon rope, dragging the cross-tie out of the woods, across the road, in front of the race car drivers hot-rod Chevrolet.

Now this all sounded like a good idea, until it actually happened! Here's what I witnessed from the front steps of Warren's house:

Warren and Corky were holding the rope on the rear side of the house. Here comes the screaming hot-rod down the street doing about eighty miles per hour.

When the timing was right, I gave Warren and Corky the signal. They started running with the rope and pulled the cross-tie across the road, right in front of the hot-rod that was passing by like a silver bullet!

The race car driver never saw Warren, Corky, or the cross-tie, before he hit it dead center with his two front wheels. I have never before or since seen anything like what I witnessed that day. It was like that hot-rod Chevrolet disintegrated, starting with the two front wheels and tearing everything out from under the car, to include the transmission and drive train.

The hot-rod had struck the cross-tie dead-center, left the ground and flew about fifty feet before nose-diving into the asphalt street.

There were car parts scattered half-way down the block and the car was completely destroyed.

It was only by the Grace of God, the driver wasn't killed!

Warren and Corky realizing what they had done, kept right on running with that cross-tie dragging behind them, for about the length of a city block. They hid the cross-tie in some woods, disconnected the rope and walked back home entering their prospective houses from the back doors, like nothing had ever happened!

Warren, Corky and myself swore an oath between us, that not one word about this incident would ever be mentioned again, and if any one of the three of us ever told what happened that day, then the other two would have permission to kill the one that talked.

Knowing that we could all end up in jail, we almost took this oath in blood!

The police came to investigate and were baffled as to what

caused all the destruction to that Chevrolet. It looked like a bomb had exploded under its hood. Even the groggy race car driver was as confused and baffled as the police.

Warren, Corky and myself went outside to see what all the commotion was about. We were acting like the other bystanders, observing the damage and looking curious, concerned and completely innocent.

As great as our acting was, all three of us knew exactly what really happened!

Mr. "Hot-Shoe" race car driver was never again observed speeding down First Street.

To this day, that massive explosion and destruction on First Street in North Jacksonville back in the 1940s still remains a mystery.

The statute of limitations has long passed. Warren's neighbor has since died, and Warren is on his last leg of life as well.

Like Paul Harvey, I guess it is safe for me to say;

"*Now you know the rest of the story!*"

More Humor:
Another humorous story that comes to mind occurred many years later, after my tour in the Air Force.

After military discharge, I secured a job with the Atlantic Coast Line Railroad, where my father, three brothers and my brother-in-law Warren worked.

Warren was an engineer, while I was assigned to the ground switching crew.

It was a clear sunny afternoon when I was called for a job, where Warren was the engineer. We had stopped our switching-train in a side track to allow a passenger-train to pass. In railroad terms, this temporary stoppage of a train crew is called being "on the spot!"

While waiting for the passenger-train, three small black-boys were walking along the railroad tracks when they stopped to talk with some of the ground crew.

I was in the engineer-cab talking with Warren, when we came up with a most ridiculous idea to have some fun with the three boys.

On a switch engine or passenger engine, there is a light-tan colored water hose which has powerful water pressure for washing down the engine deck and steps, for the safety of the switching crews.

Warren suggested that I take the water hose and feed the hose down the back side of my work-pants, between my legs and pull about six to eight inches of the hose up into my crotch area.

With this done, I walked out onto the rear platform of the engine and started talking with the three boys, who couldn't see the water hose inserted down the back of my pants.

While talking to the boys, I unzipped my fly and pulled about six inches of the hose out of the zipper-area, holding the hose as if holding my penis!

At that point, Warren who was inside the engine, turned the water valve wide-open, causing a powerful stream of water to flow from my fist which was clasped around the hose.

The water flow sprayed out about twenty-feet, which I aimed at the children, causing them to run for cover.

After about fifteen-seconds, Warren turned off the water valve. I then shook the hose a couple of times and pushed it back into my open fly, zipped it up and backed into the cab of the engine.

Warren and I were watching when the three boys walked back up to the guys on the ground crew, where we heard one of the boys say:

"That man sho can piss, can't he!"

BILLY "We must humor him" SAVAGE

*T*he meanest, most brutal, sadistic son-of-a-bitch that ever lived.

I have purposely saved this chapter on Billy and his family for last, because nobody in their right mind could believe or even comprehend the sadistic, brutal misery that this one man inflicted upon every member of the Savage family.

Billy was the first born child in the Savage family and if I didn't know my mama like I do, I'd be forced to believe that she conceived her first child directly from Satan himself!

To the reader I say; "brace yourself for the most shocking true story of domestic brutality that you have ever... or ever will read!"

Billy Savage like the rest of the male Savage clan, volunteered for the military at age seventeen, to escape the insanity of the Savage household.

Billy joined the Marines at age seventeen.

Harold joined the Army Air Force at age seventeen.

Robert joined the Navy at age seventeen.

Johnny joined the Air Force at age seventeen.

We all served a full four year enlistment with the exception of Harold, who was discharged after fifteen-months due to hardships in the family.

I remember I was nine years old and my brothers Raymond and Robert were eleven when Billy came home from the military after fighting the Japs in Okinawa for most of his four-year enlistment.

When Billy came home, my brother Harold had already moved out and had started his own family.

My mother and father still had the front bedroom. Then there was Raymond, Robert and myself in the middle bedroom and Billy now in the third bedroom. Because of the lack of space, Betty was staying at grandma's house over on the south side of Jacksonville.

When Billy returned from the war, there was one outstanding trait that he brought home with him. Billy was either "shellshocked" or just plain crazy as a damned lunatic! He was the meanest most sadistic and brutal son-of-a-bitch on the face of the earth!

Without reason or provocation, Billy's face would turn solid red and he'd take his anger out on anybody or anything within his reach.

Most of the time, Raymond, Robert and myself were the brunt of his rage, because we were always stuck in the house with him when mama and Sylvester were working.

The beatings that we suffered in that house, at the hands of Billy, would cost a man twenty-years in prison in this day and time.

Back then, it was common practice to beat the living shit out of your children. They called it discipline, but it was nothing less than total brutality of the worst order. There was no place in those days for a child to turn for help. You just took the beatings and prayed that the beater would soon get tired and stop!

When we'd tell mama how Billy was beating us half to death while she and Sylvester were at work, we always got the same response; "you children know that Billy hasn't been right since he came back from the war!" "Billy needs time to re-adjust and you're going to have to learn to humor him!"

What the hell did that mean? How do you humor a crazy, freaked out son-of-a-bitch who is three times your size, weight and age, who's beating the dog-shit out of you. What am I suppose to do, tell him a frigging joke?

With blood running down my skinny-ass legs, I guess I should say; "hey Billy, did you hear the one about the farmer's daughter …?"

Billy was completely messed-up in his head, and mama had no idea just how severe the beatings were. All we ever got for our complaints was; "you must humor Billy!" I was only nine years old, but if I had the means to get my hands on a gun, I would have humored Billy with a 38-slug right between his fucking eyes!

Billy was employed with the Atlantic Coast-Line Railroad and was working the night shift from 11:00 P.M. to 7:00 A.M.

Because us kids were alone in the house with Billy, we had to get him up at 9:00 P.M. so he could start getting ready for work.

Waking Billy was extremely dangerous! So dangerous was this task, that Raymond, Robert and myself would either draw-straws or cut-cards to see who was going to enter Billy's bedroom.

We knew that touching or shaking him from a sound sleep was about the same trauma-level as would be if a Japanese soldier came crawling into a fox-hole with Billy in the middle of the night.

I am convinced that when we tried to wake Billy, he was dreaming about the war. His first instinct and reaction was survival and fighting for his life. He would instantly swing his arm at you with such force, that it would have knocked-out Muhammad Ali on first contact.

Raymond, Robert and myself experienced some severe blows the first few times, so we tried to come up with some alternative ways to wake him.

I suggested that we poke him gently on the neck or shoulder with the end of a broom-handle. A brief discussion killed that idea because Billy would think that some Jap was poking him with the barrel of a rifle. Whoever was on the other end of that broom would surely die!

When I was low man on the card-cutting deal and had to wake Billy, here's what I'd do: I'd slip into Billy's room, step quietly up to his bed, stay as far back as I could and still reach him, calculate which direction the blow would be coming from, (based on how Billy was laying on the bed), reach out and slightly shake his arm or shoulder.

From that point on, I knew what was coming, because Billy was wired like a stick of dynamite. It was always the same. First came the lightning-fast swing of his arm. Then he would jump from the bed, grab me by both shoulders and shake me like a rag doll.

From there, his face would turn blood red, his eyes bulging almost out of their sockets, followed by a loud scream in my face:

"what in the hell do you want?" My reply was always the same; "I'm waking you up for work... it's nine o'clock!"

Billy would then release his death grip on me and I'd get my skinny-ass out of that room pronto!

That was far from the end of things however, because my brothers and I would have to set his place at the table and make damned sure his supper was hot and ready when he walked into the kitchen.

We also had to have his lunch and a thermos full of hot coffee packed neatly in his lunch-box and ready to go.

No matter how hard we tried to please or humor him as mama would say, our preparations were never good enough, and we knew that one or all of us would get the shit whipped out of us before Billy left the house.

Billy would be dressed for work and walk into the kitchen looking for any excuse to ignite into a rage.

"What is this shit?" he'd say, pointing at his supper. "This shit isn't fit for a fucking dog to eat!"

Keep in mind, that I was only nine years old and my brothers were only eleven. How well can children that age cook? We could only cook what ever Sylvester had brought into the house, which wasn't much in the first place.

It wouldn't matter if a French Chef from Paris was there cooking for Billy, he still wouldn't have been satisfied. He was so messed-up from the war, that he just wanted to hurt somebody!

Rarely did Billy eat what we had prepared for him. Instead, he would usually throw the plate of food at the wall and walk out of the house.

My brothers and I would then clean up his mess, so mama wouldn't have to face it when she got home from work at midnight.

I can remember one night after Billy threw his supper in the garbage can, he came storming into our bedroom. He was still screaming about the shit we had put on the table for his supper.

Robert and I were getting ready for bed and were standing there in our underwear, bare-chested and bare-legged. Keep in mind that Sylvester had never bought any of us a pair of pajamas.

Without warning, Billy reached into our closet and grabbed a hand full of steel coat-hangers and started beating the living hell out of Robert.

Billy had backed Robert half-way into the closet and was flailing him viciously with the coat-hangers.

Robert's legs, back and arms were blood-red with welts from the steel coat-hangers. Robert was begging Billy to stop, but he kept on and on and on slashing Robert's body and legs.

I was so concerned for Robert, that I made the grave mistake of grabbing Billy's arm. He then turned on me and started the same brutal punishment. I thought he'd never quit beating me with those coat-hangers, but he eventually stopped and walked out of the house.

My legs, back and arms were blood-red with welts and Robert was no better off. The burning pain was so great, that we went into the bathroom closet looking for something to put on the welts to help ease the burning pain.

Like everything else in our house, Sylvester's frugality only provided a jar of Vaseline to work with... and he didn't buy that for medicinal purposes!

Robert and I gently rubbed Vaseline on our bodies to no avail, trying to ease the pain. As young as I was, I still remember the welts so large, that they felt like the ridges on the metal scrubboard that mama used to do her wash.

Robert and I got into bed crying and whimpering until we finally fell asleep. The welts remained on our bodies for two or three days after that beating.

There was another time when Raymond and I were standing at the kitchen sink washing and drying dishes. Billy walked into the kitchen before leaving for work.

There was a mirror hanging on the kitchen wall, just over Raymond's head. Billy was holding a German-Lugar pistol in his hand when he said: "this is what I'm going to do to your father tonight!"

With that, Billy fired a shot that shattered the mirror into a hundred pieces! Billy then walked out of the house without another word.

My brothers and I assumed that Sylvester would meet his maker that night, but it never came off!

Billy was transferred sometime later to work a temporary railroad assignment at Ft. Pierce, Florida. While there, he met a beautiful young waitress at a restaurant where most of the railroad men ate their meals.

A few months later, Billy returned home from his railroad assignment and brought that young lady with him. Billy introduced Sarah as his wife, stating that they were married by a Justice Of The Peace at Ft. Pierce.

They remained at mama's house until a short time after their first baby was born.

Sarah was precious and was immediately accepted into the

family. Sarah was only eighteen and didn't know at the time, that this was the family of horrors, but we knew it would only be a matter of months before Billy turned her into a terrified zombie!

Billy started his marriage off with only minor fits of rage at first, but they escalated rapidly. Sarah soon learned the real side of Billy.

She never dreamed he'd sweep her off her feet, and later throw her across the room!

I'm not positive, but I believe that Billy married Sarah because he got her pregnant. I do know that it was only a few short months later, when she gave birth to her first son who they named Roger.

Roger was an innocent precious creation of God who had no way of knowing, but for his own sake, would have been better off still-born!

Roger's life from birth into adulthood would be the most torturous, abusive, miserable, physically and mentally damaging life, that any human being ever experienced!

I remember clearly when it all started. I was now about ten years old and was at the house alone with Billy, Sarah and the baby.

For some reason, Roger started to cry and didn't stop for about thirty minutes.

Anyone with a new baby knows, that this is not uncommon and is actually healthy for a new baby to exercise it's lungs.

Billy found the baby's crying most irritating. Sarah was trying everything she knew to comfort the baby and stop the crying, without success.

Billy with his ignorant philosophy thought it was time to teach his new son some discipline. Roger was only two-months old.

I remember that Billy, with his blood-red face and bulging eyes, snatched Roger from Sarah's arms. He sat down on the bed, laid the baby face down across his lap and removed the baby's diaper.

Taking a hair-brush, he turned it over to the hard-plastic side and started to slam it against the baby's fragile, palm-size butt.

Sarah and I stood there in complete shock, begging Billy to stop. Over and over, he slammed the baby's tender skin with a slap, slap, slap, slap, slap!

The baby was screaming so hard, that he lost his breath. I can still see little Roger's face even today with his mouth wide open, his face turning blue, soaked in tears, and not a sound coming out!

Billy was now in one of his killing moods and had no clue of how hard or how long he was beating this child. It was as though he was having an orgasm. The harder he beat the baby, the more he seemed to pleasure himself!

I was too scared and too small to do anything to stop Billy. Sarah had taken all she could and made the horrible mistake of grabbing Billy's arm to stop him.

With a blood-red face and veins protruding from his neck, Billy laid the baby on the bed, stood up and said to Sarah; "that is the first and last time you will ever stop me from disciplining my child!"

With that, he backed her up against the bedroom wall, drew back his arm and slammed his fist as hard as he could, right into her nose.

I remember that the back of Sarah's head was against the wall, when Billy's fist made contact. Blood flew out of her nostrils with such force, that the wall was splattered in blood on both sides of her head!

These beatings became common place. Not just for Sarah, but for all of her children which eventually numbered seven.

The children's names in order are; Roger, Tommy, Mary Lynn, Jake, Leonard, Grace and Michael.

It is most difficult for me to describe the beatings these children endured from birth through their teens, many of which I witnessed. Only God knows how many more they endured behind closed doors!

Their mother Sarah was whipped just as often, if not more.

One popular pass time antic that got Sarah many an ass-whipping, was trying to stop Billy from throwing glass baby bottles against the wall above the baby's crib.

Back in those days, there were no plastic baby bottles, ..just glass!

When Billy got tired of hearing one of his babies cry, he would take the glass bottle, and throw it as hard as he could against the wall above the head-end of the crib.

The glass bottle with milk would explode, sending shattered glass all over the baby's face and body, inside the crib.

Sarah knowing what Billy was about to do, always tried to stop him.

This only caused greater anger in Billy, who would now turn on her, and whip her until his arms got tired!

During the thirty-five plus years that Sarah was married to Billy, neither she nor the children ever enjoyed a night out for dinner, a movie, a day at the beach, a concert. Not even so much as a night at a carnival or circus ... Nothing!

All that poor woman ever got was misery and beatings. Just thinking about the life that family endured with Billy as head of the house, makes my stomach knot-up so bad, that I feel sharp pains even now as I write about the things I witnessed!

As a means of control, Billy never taught or allowed Sarah to drive a car. This way, he could keep her trapped in the house twenty-four hours a day, and that is exactly what he did.

My mind still has problems trying to comprehend what it must have been like for Sarah to be held a prisoner in her own home for thirty-five years.

None of Billy's children had it any better. From birth to their teens, they were forced to stay either inside the house or no further than to play in the fenced back yard. Once reaching school age, they were ordered to come directly home from school and stay in the house.

They were never allowed to go to school functions or have any personal friends.

They never attended a football game, sports-rally or prom. Not one of them ever had a sweetheart, or "puppy-love" affair. They, just like their mother, only knew confinement, intimidation and beatings.

Their house was totally and perpetually void of laughter or love.

Billy's children were so ignorant through no fault of their own, that they had no inkling, even in their early teens, how to ride a public bus, how much to pay the driver for their ride, or even how to go shopping.

Billy would drink whole-milk and always ate well, while his seven children drank-powdered milk. Food in Billy's household was similar to what I remembered when I was a child in Sylvester's house.

The children knew better than to complain about the milk, food or anything else for that matter. When Billy was home, they kept their mouths shut and stayed out of his way.

A good example is that of Billy's first-born son Roger. He's the one who suffered the severe beating with a hair-brush when he was two-months old.

Roger was so afraid of Billy, that he wouldn't speak or make any noise when Billy was in the house, for fear that he would be whipped.

Roger just sat in the corner of the living room or in his bedroom, which he shared with his brothers, never making a sound.

Dear God, I hate to write this, but little Roger never spoke a single word until he was five years old. Yes, he could make sounds, because he screamed every day from his beatings, but never actually spoke a legible word.

When Roger was six years old and enrolled in public-school, he had to be placed in a special speech-therapy class for the deaf & dumb, even though there was nothing physically wrong with his vocal-cords.

He was just too frightened to speak or make any noise, that might bring on a whipping. That is how Roger perceived it. Make any noise or speak, and you automatically receive a beating. Keep quiet, and you may survive!

I remember when Roger was twelve-years old. Mama took him from his house one day while Billy was at work, walked with him to a city bus-stop, got on the bus, dropped their token into the change receptacle and rode to downtown Jacksonville.

Mama was determined to teach little Roger how to ride a city bus and how to go shopping. They spent the entire day going from one store to another. They had lunch at the counter of a Five & Dime Store, went to a movie and then rode the bus home again.

This was the most enjoyable and exciting day Roger had ever spent!

Mama then set out to take Sarah downtown shopping, but Sarah kept saying that she didn't want to go. Mama finally forced Sarah to tell her why she wouldn't go shopping, when mama was going to pay for everything.

Sarah finally admitted to mama; "because I know you'll want me to try on some clothes, and I'm embarrassed!"

After some pressuring from mama, Sarah said; "I don't have one pair of feminine underwear, no bra or panties!"

Mama and Sarah were in the house alone at the time and mama demanded that Sarah lift her skirt and show her what she was wearing. Reluctantly Sarah lifted her skirt. Mama was shocked and angry at what she saw. She felt so badly for Sarah, that she cried.

Sarah was wearing a pair of Billy's boxer shorts which were lapped over at her waist and pinned with a safety-pin.

Now you have to picture this; Billy weighed approximately three-hundred-fifty pounds, and Sarah weighed approximately one-hundred-fifteen pounds. The waist overlap was a good twelve inches. The legs were at least three times larger than Sarah's, and the hems of the boxer shorts hung all the way past her knees. Sarah had no bra!

Mama dressed Sarah up as best she could and took her to town shopping. Mama bought her several bras and two dozen panties, to include some other articles of both house clothes and dress clothes.

When Billy came in from work and saw the new clothes, Sarah caught hell. Billy thought that Sarah went crying to mama about her needs, when in fact, she had not!

I used to worry about Sarah's children, and on occasion would ride my motor-scooter around to Billy's house to see them. I always knew that I could find them in the back-yard, since that was the only place they were ever allowed to go.

I rode up on my motor-scooter and parked it next to the driveway. Billy's children heard me, and without thinking, came running out of the back yard to greet me.

They loved me, like I loved them and they were so excited to see me, especially the boys. They wanted to see my motor-scooter, since they never were around anything like that.

The excitement made the children forget, that they weren't allowed outside the chain-link fence of the back yard, so here they came running and shouting, "Uncle Johnny"… "Uncle Johnny!"

Billy was inside the house and heard the commotion. Out he came with a hard-plastic baseball-bat in his hand. The children saw Billy and at the same moment realized the mistake they had made. They all tried to turn and run back, but Billy was blocking them.

Little Tommy was terrified because he couldn't run as fast as the others. He was born with a serious rupture to his scrotum which severely limited his mobility.

Gripping the bat with both hands, Billy started swinging. He caught some of the children with a full force blow, knocking them to the ground.

I remember poor little Tommy, almost made it past Billy, while he was striking some of the others, but Billy rotated his body and caught him full force in the middle of his back, knocking him about six feet forward onto his face and chest.

Billy had knocked the breath out of Tommy and he was lying on the ground gasping for air. I picked Tommy up to his feet and blocked Billy from striking him again, until Tommy finally caught a breath of air and started crying. He stumbled on into the back yard.

I was so upset and hurt, that I just got back on my motor-scooter and rode away. I don't know what else he did to them after I left.

My eyes were full of tears and I was devastated with anger. I wished to God that I was old enough and strong enough to go back, rescue those children and kill that no good rotten son-of-a-bitch, who was pretending to be a father!

This is the same Billy who joined a Baptist Church around the corner from his house and volunteered to be an usher. He would stand at the front entry, greet every member and visitor with a firm hand shake and say: "Good Morning", "God Bless You", "How Are You?" or "Jesus Loves You."

All the while, still having traces of dried blood on his knuckles that came from his wife's nose.

BILLY THE NIGGER KILLER

Our house never had, nor had we ever heard of a thing called air-conditioning.

The days in Jacksonville were blistering hot and the nights were unbearable.

Thank God we had screens on our windows, so we could leave them open to allow some resemblance of air flow at night while we tried to sleep.

Within an hour of retiring for the night, our bed-sheets would be soaking wet from perspiration.

We didn't worry about burglars or security like people do in this day and time. We had too many other problems on our minds.

I remember one summer night, just before midnight, we heard our next door neighbor scream; "Mrs. Savage, there's a nigger man looking in your bedroom window!"

As soon as we heard our neighbor screaming that a nigger was looking in the bedroom window, mama screamed back..."okay, I'm calling the police!"

Our neighbor who lived on the second floor of the old shotgun-house next door, was sitting on her front porch late, because it was too hot to sleep.

She reported that a nigger teenager had rode up on his bicycle, leaned it against a telephone-pole on the sidewalk area and crept down the dirt-alley to look into mama's bedroom window, where she was reading, and still had her light on.

The " peeping-tom" teenager had run off on foot… too scared to go back for his bicycle with all the screaming and commotion going on.

The police came and made a report, saying that their patrol units were looking for any nigger on foot, this time of night!

The police were going to take the bicycle away, when my sadistic brother Billy, asked them if they would leave it for a while.

Billy told the cops that he was positive the nigger would come back and try to retrieve his bicycle, because to any teenager, white or black in those days, a bicycle was a valuable possession.

The cop laughed and said; "you're gonna lay low and catch you a nigger." I know what you're gonna do!"

Billy said; "leave the bike, and I'll deliver you one hurtin nigger before this night is over!"

The cop said; "have at it!", while they laughed and drove away. The bike was still leaning against the telephone-pole, when Billy told all of us to go to bed, turn off the lights and be quiet!

Billy dressed in some dark-coveralls, took my baseball bat out of the hall closet, went outside and hid in some bushes a few feet from the bike, and waited there for about two hours.

Most of us were asleep, when we heard all hell break loose outside.

I never heard so much pounding, screaming and pleading in all my life.

The screaming went on for several minutes before it got deadly quiet!

Mama called the police again before we all ran to the front porch to see what had happened.

It didn't take long for the police to respond, and it didn't take long for all the on-lookers to see what Billy had done to this young man.

The neighbors were shouting, "Billy got the nigger!... Billy got the nigger!"

Someone shouted out; "the nigger came back for his bicycle, just like Billy said he would!"

I was really scared, but I took a good look at that bloody mess lying there in the dirt. There was no movement what-so-ever, and I was positive the young man was dead. Billy was still holding the baseball-bat and walking around like a proud barnyard rooster!

The police couldn't detect any sign of life in the remains of that battered carcass, and believe it or not, they threw the body and the bicycle in the back of a police paddy-wagon and drove away.

The detective that came, said they would take the "boy" to the hospital and see if there was anything that could be done. He told Billy not to worry about anything, that it was obvious to the police, that this was a case of *self-defense!*

If there was ever any kind of hearing or inquiry, I never heard about it. I do know that Billy made some kind of report, and that was the end of it!

Billy bragged for years about killing his nigger!

BILLY "THE LANDSCAPE ARTIST"

Mama was always concerned for the welfare and safety of Sarah and her children, so she would stop by unannounced on occasion, to see what was going on and to see if Sarah and the children had adequate food in the house.

Billy only lived a few blocks from mama's house and on one occasion when mama walked around there, she found that Billy's front and back lawn was grown-up to about knee level to the children.

Sarah told mama that Billy had been working just about every day for the last three weeks and hadn't had time to mow the lawn.

Feeling sorry for the children who had no place to play but in the back yard, mama could just see a snake striking one of the children, if the lawn and weeds weren't cut. She asked Sylvester if he would go around there and cut the front and back lawn.

Sylvester took his mower around to Billy's house and cut the lawn before he went to work. My parents were both working from 3:00 P.M. to 11:00 P.M.

Billy came home from work at 4:00 P.M. and demanded to

know who cut his lawn. Billy hated Sylvester, so when he found out that Sylvester had cut his lawn; he flew into a massive rage!

Billy loaded every garden and lawn tool that he owned into his car, to include chains, rope, power-saw and an ax.

He then drove around to mama's house and started his landscape artistry on her trees, shrubs, flowers, plants and St. Augustine grass.

Now before I tell you about Billy's landscape artistry, you must know this: Mama and Sylvester were now in their senior years, and living in the house that mama had originally bought many years ago, when she and us children tried to escape from Sylvester.

Mama and Sylvester took great pride in their lawn, trees and shrubs.

Their landscape was beautiful and the flowers were in full bloom.

There were two beautiful Palms on the front lawn and a number of well-pruned trees on the back lawn. Both sides of mama's house were lined in beautiful boxed shrubs.

Billy unloaded his car and started to work on mama's landscape. He first took his chain saw and cut down the Palm-trees, the fruit-trees and all the shrubs on both sides of the house.

Anything that was too large to cut and move, Billy chained to the bumper of his car and pulled out of the ground.

He then recklessly drove his car all over the lawn trying to destroy the expensive St. Augustine grass, and crushing all the flowers.

He then loaded up his tools and drove back around to his house.

When mama and Sylvester arrived home about the same time at midnight, they both thought a tornado had passed through the neighborhood, destroying their property. They could see no damage to their neighbor's lawns, because it was past midnight and too dark to really see.

The next A.M., they went back outside and couldn't believe

their eyes. Everything they had worked on for so many years was destroyed, and not one blade of grass was damaged in the neighbor's yards.

Mama walked over to her next-door neighbor to ask her if she knew what happened and if a tornado had passed through. The neighbor told mama that a tornado had passed through all right, and it's name was Billy!

The neighbor was an elderly lady who told mama that she was afraid of Billy, like everybody else, and that she was helpless to do anything but to stand looking out of her living room window watching, while Billy destroyed mama's lawn and landscape.

It took mama and Sylvester years to restore and re-plant their property, but they eventually got it done at great expense.

As for Billy, not one word was said to him, as mama heeded to her own advise, and decided to keep quiet and humor Billy!

With all his meanness, Billy became a member of a local Baptist Church near his home. He even became an usher and greeted people at the front door!

This was a big joke to me and everyone else. We couldn't understand how a man could play the part of a good Christian follower, and then go straight home and beat the living shit out of his wife and children. What a hypocrite!

Billy was quick to volunteer his children to mow, cut and clean the Church property on a regular basis.

He even loaned out his children to care for the pastor's personal property.

That pastor would work those children all day long on a Saturday, never feed them a bite, and then make them walk home, because they were too dirty to ride in his car.

One Saturday afternoon, all seven of Billy's children were walking past mama's house on their way home, when mama called out to them to stop. They told her they had been working all day on the pastor's property.

Mama soon found out that they hadn't eaten all day, and

brought them into the house, cleaned them up and fed them until their bellies were full!

When mama later complained to Billy about this, he responded by saying; "a little manual labor won't kill them!"

Billy then had the balls to make the following statement to mama: "my preacher told me that I should take the television away from the kids, because it will corrupt their minds and fill their heads with evil!"

Hearing Billy say that, caused mama to go totally berserk! I was lucky enough to be standing there when she jumped in Billy's face and screamed: "I dare you to take the television from those babies,… I just dare you!" "Television is the only contact they have with the real world!" "I don't give a damn what that preacher had to say about those babies watching their shows, I just dare you to take it away!"

Mama then went on screaming; "those babies have absolutely no recreation what-so-ever. They're never allowed to go anywhere or do anything, and you have the gall to stand there and even consider taking away their television… I just dare you… I dare you!"

This was the first time mama didn't humor Billy!

I don't remember ever seeing mama with such anger and fury as I witnessed that day. Needless to say, their television wasn't taken away.

Although Sylvester eventually became a member of that same church in his senior years, mama went to church elsewhere, and never had anything to do with Sylvester's pastor.

There came a time when that pastor asked mama why she so disliked him, and that was a serious mistake on his part. Mama told him she couldn't sit there listening to him preach out of both sides of his mouth at the same time.

She was referring to his treatment of Billy's children in the past, and then to have the gall to stand there in the pulpit preaching the good word!

Enough said. God could punish me now, for my comments on this man of the cloth. *Forgive me Lord!*

BILLY'S "REPOSSESSION SERVICE"

In Billy's back yard, there was an old abandoned 1949 Mercury Two-Door Coupe. Billy had parked and abandoned the old car years ago, as not worthy to repair.

Billy's children used the old car as a playhouse. The car had no windows, the upholstery was completely weather worn, the tires were rotted and flat and the floor was ankle deep in sand.

Cars built in those days were made of solid steel, so the rust had not yet taken over the car.

Robert came up with a good idea, to completely restore the old car for his main transportation. In those days, the 1949 Mercury Coupe was a popular body style with the teenagers and collectors. Dropping the rear-end about four inches, fender-skirts and a dual glass-pack exhaust system was the thing.

Robert offered Billy two-hundred dollars for the old junk car and Billy was eager to accept the cash, if Robert would pay to have the car hauled out of Billy's back yard.

Robert bought the car, received the title and a bill of sale before hiring a wrecker to haul the car out of the yard. The car was then delivered to a local auto restoration shop, where Robert ordered the complete works. New upholstery, new glass, new wheels, new tires, a complete engine overhaul, and five coats of black-lacquer paint.

Robert's restored black-beauty cost him over two-thousand dollars.

The same restoration at today's price would cost a good ten-thousand dollars.

After two months in restoration, Robert was driving his custom beauty around Jacksonville. It looked like it just rolled off the show room floor. Robert was one proud human being, and I really envied him!

Robert was still living with mama and Sylvester at that time, working for the railroad on the night shift.

Less than sixty-days after the car restoration, Robert was sleeping one day in his back bedroom, when Billy entered the house with his pass key. Mama allowed Billy to have a key to her front door because he was always raiding her refrigerator, freezer or pantry for food to feed his children. Billy cried poor-mouth twenty-four hours a day, to anybody that would listen.

Billy crept quietly into Robert's bedroom and started searching through Robert's pants pockets, which were hanging on the closet door.

The rustling sounds of the unauthorized search woke Robert up, where he sat straight up in bed.

"What are you doing with your hands in my pants pockets?" Robert demanded!

Billy responded; "I want the keys to my car, and I want them now!"

Robert said; "I don't have the keys to your car, so get the hell out of my room!"

Billy said; "I'm going to ask you one last time, to give me the keys to my fucking Mercury, and give them to me now!"

Robert said; "I don't have keys to *your* Mercury, the Mercury is *mine!*"

The next thing Robert knew, Billy was straddling his chest, and had a knife-blade pressed against Robert's throat.

With a fire-red face, Billy screamed into Robert's face saying; : "If you don't give me the keys to my Mercury right now, I'm going to cut your fucking throat from ear-to-ear, and you know I'll do it!"

Robert laid very still and said; "the keys are in the top-drawer of my dresser!"

Billy crawled off Robert's chest, took the car keys and drove away in Robert's Mercury.

Robert hitched a ride to work that night, and the next morning he confronted mama and Sylvester about what had happened.

Robert told mama and Sylvester that he was going to file criminal charges against Billy for threatening his life with a knife, and for stealing his Mercury.

Mama started begging and pleading with Robert not to call the police.

"If you call the police and have Billy arrested, he'll lose his job with the railroad, then what would Sarah and the children do?"

"If Billy loses his job and goes to jail, Sarah and the children will be the ones to suffer!"

In those days, working for the railroad was a premium job, that was most sought after. If arrested or convicted of a criminal offense, a railroad employee would be fired in a heart-beat!

And then came those horrid, dreaded words once again out of mama's mouth, that we had heard so many times before: "you must learn to humor Billy… he has never been right since he came back from the war!"

Robert humored Billy one last time by signing over the Mercury title and registration.

Robert packed his belongings and moved to Atlanta, ending any future contact with Billy again.

The next time that Robert looked into Billy's face, it was facing upward from inside a casket.

BILLY'S BURNED BUTTER BEANS

The rain was coming down so hard, it looked like sheets of water. I was watching it from the living room window when the phone rang.

The caller was Billy's wife, Sarah. I could tell by her voice that she was in a panic. She was trying to tell me something, and crying at the same time.

"Johnny, is anybody there with you?" Sarah pleaded.

"No I answered, I'm here alone!"

"Johnny, do you know anybody that has a car, that you can call?"

I told Sarah that I didn't know anyone to call.

Sarah told me that before Billy went to bed, he told her to have a pot of butter-beans cooked when he got up. (Large lima beans are what southerners call butter-beans.)

Billy was working the night shift at the railroad, so he slept during the day.

Sarah had started cooking a pot of dried butter-beans about two hours before she was to awaken Billy. She then bathed her children and got them ready for bed. Forgetting the beans on the stove, all the water had boiled out, and Billy's precious butter-beans were now burned and stuck to the bottom of the pot!

Sarah knew that when she got Billy up for work and told him that his butter-beans were burned, she would get a vicious whipping!

In desperation, she was hoping that someone could get another bag of dried lima beans to her, so she could cook them before Billy got up.

I wasn't that much of a cook, but I had enough sense to know that it takes about an hour and a half to cook a pot of dried beans.

I remembered that mama always soaked her dried beans for a couple of hours before cooking them.

I explained this to Sarah, reminding her that she had to get Billy up in less than an hour.

I was thirteen and only had my motor scooter. With the massive rain and hard winds, there was no way that I could make the trip to the supermarket and get a bag of beans to Sarah in time. I'm not even sure if I had the money to buy them anyway.

Sarah was still crying when she hung up.

As I look back now, I wish there was something I could have done, even if it meant walking three miles in that rain, to get Sarah a bag of dried beans. Just as Sarah had said, Billy got up and turned into a raging bull when she told him the beans were burned.

Sarah later told mama that she knew there was nothing she could do, but stand there and brace herself for the full-contact blow of Billy's fist to her face.

Sarah and her children were so used to getting the shit beat out of them, that they just braced for the impact and prayed to God for the best. They were helpless against Billy's rage, and had no one to defend them.

The worst thing about Billy's beatings, was that he never knew when to stop. It was like he was going through an out of body experience, where his mind was someplace else, and he lost all consciousness of what he was doing! Only God knows how many, or the severity of the beatings that Sarah and those children had taken over the years.

The only way out for several of the children was suicide!

SARAH'S HEMORRHAGE

I hate to think what horrifying deviate sexual torture that Sarah must have endured from Billy behind closed doors. I know that he was a perverted ass-hole, so I can only imagine what his sick mind could come up with and what things he did to that poor woman!

I say this because I can remember when I was about twelve years old, Billy and Sarah rented one of the shotgun houses, directly across the street from mama's house, for about a year.

Mama and I were sitting on the front porch one day, when we both heard Sarah screaming; "mama", "mama" , "mama", as she came running across the street toward our house.

I remember that Sarah was wearing a dress that was soaked in blood from her hips to the hem. She also had blood running down her legs into her shoes!

Mama jumped up and helped Sarah into our house, taking her to the bathroom and laying her on the floor, so she could examine Sarah's vaginal area, and try to stop the hemorrhaging!

I was standing in the bathroom doorway watching in horror, when I heard mama ask Sarah what caused this? I remember that Sarah started to say; "Billy made me … … ….!"

Then mama looked up and saw me standing there. Mama told me to go sit on the front-porch and she closed the bathroom door so I couldn't hear what Billy made Sarah do.

I was young and dumb and knew little to nothing about sex, and boy was I curious as to what Billy could have done to cause all this.

I knew that Billy did something horrible, but never did find out what.

Mama took care of the hemorrhage and Sarah returned to Billy's house of horror!

A REAL MAN STOOD UP TO BILLY

I was eleven years old when I spotted a For-Sale sign, on a used Cushman Motor Scooter parked at an Amoco Service Station on the corner of Lake Shore Boulevard and Casset Avenue.

I walked into the station and ask the manager how much he wanted for the motor scooter. "One-hundred-twenty-five dollars!" grumbled the manager!

Now that man knew damned well that some skinny-ass eleven year old kid didn't have that kind of money, so he didn't want me taking up his time.

"Does it run pretty good?" I asked!

"It runs real good boy! ... you got that kind of money?", he asked.

I quickly said: "no sir, but I'll save it up, if you'll hold it for me!"

"Well it's for sale to the first person that hands me the money!" replied the manager.

God meant for me to have that motor scooter, because I felt it in my heart.

For income, I was sacking groceries for tips at the local A&P

Supermarket after school. On weekends I sold newspapers down town.

Between the two jobs, I could drum up about fifteen dollars a week, if I put in a lot of hours and saved every cent.

I remember that I had a total of eighteen dollars in my pocket when I first walked back to that Amoco Station and asked the manager, if he would take the eighteen dollars as a deposit to hold the motor scooter.

"You really want that motor scooter bad, don't you boy?"

"Yes sir, I want that scooter so bad I can taste it!"

"Tell you what boy, I believe you'll honor your word, so here's what I'm gonna do:"

The station manager proceeded to tell me that he'd lock the scooter up in the shed behind the station, and that he'd hold it for six-weeks. If I didn't have the one-hundred-twenty-five dollars by then, he'd sell it to somebody else.

I don't know why he agreed to do that for me. I can only guess that God had a hand in guiding his decision!

To meet the deadline, I worked my skinny fingers to the bone for the next six weeks and saved every cent I made.

I remember clearly one day that my brother Billy came into my room and saw me counting my money, which I kept in an old cigar box, in the bottom of my underwear drawer.

Billy asked me what I was doing with that money, and I told him what I was saving it for.

Billy said to me: "It's not safe to keep your money in your underwear drawer, so why don't you let me keep it for you?" "When you save up enough, I'll give it to you, so you can buy your scooter?"

I gave Billy my cigar box with my money for safekeeping.

Every week, I gave him my fifteen to twenty dollars to keep for me.

The six weeks finally came, but it seemed more like six years. I was worried to death, that the station manager might have forgotten me, and sold the scooter to someone else.

I can remember when the day came, that I had the final twenty dollars. This gave me a grand-total of one-hundred-twenty-eight dollars that I had saved.

This was enough to pay for the scooter, change the oil and fill her up with gas. Boy was I ever ready to go and get my scooter!

I was so proud when I ran to my brother Billy, and with great glowing excitement asked him for my money.

I would rather that Billy had stabbed me in the heart, than to hear his reply: "you don't need no damned motor scooter, you'll just get yourself killed!"

I said to Billy: "please give me my money, cause if I don't pay the man today, he'll sell it to somebody else!"

Billy said: "I don't give a shit if he does sell it to somebody else,

I'm not giving you the money... so shut up about it!"

I realized then, that Billy had spent my money, and never had any intention of safekeeping it in the first place. Oh God, what a fool I had been to trust Billy, knowing the evil he possessed!

I sat on the front porch not knowing what to do, when my brother-in-law Warren drove up. Now Warren was much of a man who grew up on a Georgia farm and could whip a wildcat barehanded.

Warren saw that I was crying and asked me what was wrong.

I told him what had happened, and that Billy wouldn't give me my money.

Warren knew, just like everybody else, that Billy was a no good son-of-a-bitch. There was no love lost between those two, even before this incident!

To my surprise, Warren said to me: "go get in my car, we're going to get your motor scooter right now!"

We drove to the Amoco Service Station, where Warren somehow satisfied the manager about the one-hundred-twenty-five dollars, filled my motor scooter with gas, and followed me home in his car.

Before I rode away from the station, Warren squatted down

beside me and said: "I covered for your scooter, because I'm not gonna let Billy steal your money!" "Consider this a loan Johnny, because Billy now owes me the one-hundred-twenty-five dollars and I guarantee you... he *will* pay me!"

I remember that wonderful feeling when I cranked up that scooter, thanked the manager and started riding home. The wind blowing through my hair felt like I was running ninety miles an hour, when I was probably not doing much more than twenty-five.

When we arrived back home, Billy was in his bedroom. Warren walked to the bedroom door, with me following in his shadow.

Warren said: "Billy, you owe me one-hundred-twenty-five dollars, and I want my money now!"

Billy replied: "how in hell do you think that I owe you one-hundred twenty-five dollars?"

Warren answered: "because I loaned Johnny one-hundred-twenty five dollars for his motor scooter and he told me I could collect the money that you're holding for him!"

Billy said: "well that's tough shit, cause I told Johnny that he couldn't have the damned motor scooter and that's the end of it!"

Warren countered: "the end of it will be when I take the money out of your damned ass!" "If you don't hand me my money, you're gonna get the ass whipping of your life... do you understand me?"

I guess Billy clearly understood, cause he handed Warren the money. I was happy to have my scooter, but I guess it might have been worth the loss, to see Warren whip the shit out of Billy!

That was the first time I ever saw anybody face Billy down.

It's clear to me as I look back now, Billy never intimidated anyone but women and children. I just had never seen him try to inflict his rage on a real man before.

I'll remember forever, the day a real man stood up for a grieving, mentally whipped and intimidated eleven year old child.

Thank you Warren.

SYLVESTER CAN'T LEAVE WELL ENOUGH ALONE

You may have asked yourself by now; "how long did Sylvester keep his Mr. Macho-Man shit up, or did he ever quit acting like a fool?"

Brace yourself for Sylvester's final episode at age seventy-five!

Sylvester and mama were now living together in their senior years, but in separate bedrooms. Robert was still living at home.

Sylvester slept in the front bedroom... mama slept in the middle bedroom... and Robert slept in the back bedroom.

Mama hadn't slept in the same room with Sylvester in more than twenty-five years. Because of the horrible things that he did to her and the way he treated her in the past, she couldn't stand him near her.

Old Sylvester was starting to get a little senile and his mind was playing tricks on him. Suddenly he got it in his head that mama was his woman and by God, she was going to be in his bed, whether she liked it or not!

Sylvester walked to mama's bedroom where she had already

retired for the night, and demanded that she get up and bring her ass to his bed... and that was his terminology!

Mama laughed at Sylvester and told him; "go to bed old man and leave me alone!"

Nothing would do, but for mama to get out of her bed and get into his bed and he didn't mean maybe!

Mama got out of bed, slammed and locked her bedroom door in Sylvester's face, which set-off his temper big time!

Sylvester started slamming his fists into mama's bedroom door with all the power he had, demanding that she open the door and come to his bed.

Mama just laughed and said; ... "you'd better get your fat-ass away from my door and go to bed!"

By this time, Robert had come out of his bedroom and asked what the hell was going on?

Mama shouted at Robert, to go back into his bedroom, so that he wouldn't get hurt, in case Sylvester succeeded in breaking down her door.

Mama didn't have to tell Robert twice, because he knew that "Ma-Barker" was about to surface, just like the "Incredible-Hulk" would do on television!

Mama then shouted at Sylvester; "you know I have a pistol under my bed old man, so if you don't get your ass away from my door and go to bed, you'll be spending tonight in the morgue!"

Hearing mama's warning, Robert opened his door one more time, and cautioned Sylvester of the extreme danger. He then locked himself in his bedroom, leaving Sylvester still standing at mama's bedroom door, ranting and raving.

Sylvester started banging on mama's door again, shouting for her to open the door and service her husbands needs, that it was her duty as a wife!

Sylvia "Ma-Barker" came to life, got her gun out from under the bed, and fired four rounds through the bedroom door!

How in the hell she missed Sylvester is still a mystery today, because mama fired all four shots through the center of the door.

I believe that Sylvester must have been standing to one side while beating his fists on the door, when the shots were fired.

Sylvester ran as fast as he could to his own bedroom and locked the door behind him.

Mama never did open her door to see if Sylvester was lying dead in the hall. She just turned out her lights and went to sleep!

Robert who was already a basket-case, just laid quietly in his bed until morning.

When the sun came up, Robert looked out in the hall, and found wood splinters from mama's door scattered from one end of the hall to the other!

There was no sign of Sylvester's body, so Robert assumed he was still alive somewhere.

Sylvester didn't mess with mama's head ever again after that. He died about six-years later of a heart-attack and not a tear was shed at his funeral!

There was always something going on in the Savage household to include fist-fighting, knife-fighting, gun-shots, screaming, cursing, threats and intimidation.

From the day I was born, until the day I moved out, this was just a way of life for us. God only knows what horrors took place before I came along!

Being the youngest of six, I asked mama why she stayed in this marriage. Mama said that in those days, there was no place that a woman with six children could go for help. That couples stayed together, regardless of the mental or physical abuses in their marriage.

Mama said that if she had left Sylvester, all the children would have ended up in foster homes. She chose to endure hell on earth, to keep the family together.

SCREAM OF DEATH

One of mama's best friends was a neighbor named Mrs. Kingston, who lived just a few doors away. Mama and Mrs. Kingston were about the same age and had been neighbors for more than fifty years.

On one calm Sunday morning, Mrs. Kingston and her husband Sonny, were sitting at the kitchen table, when an argument erupted.

Sonny Kingston was always on edge and ready to explode, when anything was said or happened that rubbed him the wrong way. He wasn't a well man. He suffered with high blood pressure and extremely frayed nerves.

Anything slightly out of the norm would set Sonny into a tirade. This man looked for anything to start an argument and upset his wife.

Married to and living with Sonny for more than fifty-five years, Mrs. Kingston knew to ignore his rampages and to do everything possible to appease him and head off arguments.

While eating his breakfast, Sonny looked across the table at his wife and said; "I saw an article on the news last night, that said people with bad nerves, should find an outlet to vent their frustrations!"

"The psychologist on the show said one way to vent the anger and frustration, is to scream at the top of your lungs!"

"Screaming is like a pressure valve popping off a boiler, it lets the steam out!"

After Sonny made these comments, and without any warning, he leaned across the table toward his wife, and with all the power in his lungs, he opened his mouth and screamed directly into her face.

Sonny relieved his pressure, but the shock was so great to his wife, that she suffered a massive stroke and dropped dead while sitting at the kitchen table! Sonny died of grief three months later. Mama, Robert and myself attended both funerals.

ROBERT NEVER SEES THE DOCTOR

Robert never visits any doctors. He is sixty-eight years of age, and to my knowledge, hasn't seen a doctor more than two or three times since he left the Navy at age 21.

When I say doctor, I mean any kind of doctor. No general practitioner, no specialist, no dentist, no eye exams, no nothing.

God knows what his prostate or colon looks like. I pleaded with Robert to at least visit the doctor for a prostate exam, explaining that men over forty, should have this checked for cancer at least twice a year.

Robert said; "I ain't letting no doctor stick his finger up my ass, cancer or not!"

Robert brushes his teeth three or four times a day, but will not visit a dentist.

Robert has never had his eyes examined in his sixty-eight years on this earth. He desperately needs glasses, but refuses to go for an eye exam.

About once a year, he goes to Walgreen's Drug Store and purchases a stronger pair of magnification glasses for about twelve-dollars. He has elevated to their most powerful pair, and still cannot read small print.

His cheap glasses are always held together with paper-clip wire, or wrapped in white medical tape.

He has now resorted to a large "Sherlock Holmes" hand held magnifying glass, so he can read the newspaper!

I tried to explain to Robert, that prescription glasses would not only allow him to see, but it will help to correct his vision levels by strengthening both eyes to the same vision levels.

Robert just replies as always, "don't worry about me, I see just fine!"

It's not a matter of money that keeps Robert from the doctors, because mama has offered to pay for his doctor visit and the prescription glasses. He is just stubborn and too set in his ways, to change now!

Robert has started losing massive weight, and looks like he just walked out of a German Prison Camp of World-War Two.

He has serious pain in his legs and back. He walks with a walker, and sleeps most of the time.

Robert hasn't left Mama's house in more than a year, and still refuses to let a doctor examine him.

I have consulted a medical doctor and both the doctor and I agree that all the symptoms could possibly indicate stomach or colon cancer!

Robert's OCD problem has worsened over the years to a point that he washes his hands every few minutes, all day long. His wrists and hands are completely raw and on occasion bleed.

Robert applies lotion to his hands and then washes them again every few minutes. No lotion or medication will help, because he washes it off shortly after application!

Robert continues to go through full cases of paper-towels every two or three weeks.

He has reached a point that he won't touch anything without a paper towel or napkin in his hand.

Robert walks around with a napkin in both of his hands every minute that he isn't sleeping. He opens the kitchen cabinets with napkins in his hand. The same goes for touching the TV-controls, opening a door, turning on the water faucets, or answering the phone. He even picks up his plate or drinking glass with a napkin in his hand.

Since mama and Robert both are too sick to get out of the house anymore, I do all their grocery shopping every two or three weeks. Their shopping list always includes the full case of paper-towels, and now includes a package of 500 paper-napkins.

Robert will sit at the kitchen table for hours, cutting each paper-napkin into four squares.

He then uses the squares of paper to carry in his hands all day long.

Walking around mama's house, you will find stacks of the paper-napkins on the kitchen table, on the kitchen counters, on top of the TV set next to the front door, on the bathroom counter, on all the end tables in every bedroom, and even in the garage next to the refrigerator/freezer!

No germ will ever touch Robert's raw, bloody hands!

Robert will die many years before his time from some medical problem that could have been detected and cured. Either that, or he will mentally and emotionally go off the deep-end!

I pray for Robert every day!

ROBERT'S WEATHER ALMANAC 2005

If it isn't enough to put up with Robert's other obsessive (OCD) behavior, he has now developed a new routine that is driving mama and me crazy.

Since Robert hasn't left the house (other than when I take him for a haircut) in more than three years, he has run out of things to occupy his mind. He now has adopted a massive interest in the daily TV weather broadcasts.

From sun up until sundown, Robert listens to the weather broadcasts. He records every weather broadcast prediction for the city where he lives, on pieces of napkin paper. He cuts up hundreds of napkins in four squares that he uses to record weather reports.

Sitting at the kitchen table, he intensely watches televised weather forecasts over and over all day long, recording every temperature and weather change on these napkins. He then stacks the filled out napkins in neat stacks on the kitchen table where they permanently remain.

I visit Robert and mama every twelve days (three-hundred miles round trip) making sure their bills are paid and they have adequate food & medications. I also take this time to complete any house maintenance and other needs such as changing filters, etc!

The first thing I see when I walk into the house, is this gigantic stack of napkins with months of weather forecasts & predictions.

I usually stay over for two or three days to visit and take care of things. It just really gets on my nerves, when I am trying to watch a good television show like "24" or "Law & Order", to have Robert keep interrupting my concentration with his outbursts of another weather or temperature report!

Mama is now 96 years of age, and Robert will be 70 next December. The three of us are all that's left of the family, so I bite my lip or take a Valium to control my blood-pressure. I love them regardless, and want to spend as much time taking care of them as my nerves will permit.

God, give me strength.

DOLLAR-WEED INFESTATION CAN BE HAZARDOUS

A few years back, when mama & Robert were still getting around, she absolutely loved working and caring for her lawn.

At ninety-three years of age, mama still found a way to oversee the care of her lawn and shrubs. Her St. Augustine grass was always healthy and weed free.

One day she noticed a serious dollar-weed problem in her next door neighbor's lawn!

Mama spent her days worrying about the status of Robert's soul and salvation. The rest of the day, she worried about her lawn, while watching TV weather reports.

Mama could still walk, but only with extreme care and patience. She managed a daily walk to the front door, so she could look out and view the condition of her lawn and shrubs.

Mama sent word of warning to her next door neighbor, that his lawn had a serious dollar-weed problem. That he should take immediate steps to rid his lawn of this problem, and that he should mow his lawn on a more regular basis.

Mama tried to explain to her neighbor, that if he didn't rid his lawn of the dollar-weed, that it would spread rapidly over to her lawn, and would infest and destroy her beautiful St. Augustine grass.

Now this neighbor didn't know mama, or her reputation as a woman of few words, so he just ignored the advise of this old lady and went on about his business.

Mama waited two months before she decided to take action. All the while, making my brother Robert, pull the creeping, nasty dollar-weed by it's roots, with his bare hands.

When Robert complained, mama would say; "If we don't stop the growth of our neighbor's dollar-weed, it will crawl over on my lawn and destroy my beautiful St. Augustine grass!"

Now for those of you who don't know what St. Augustine grass is, it's the most expensive and sought after lawn covering in the south!

Robert was fighting a losing battle, because for every basket of dollar-weed he pulled, twice that amount would grow back in a few days.

Like the "Incredible Hulk", "Ma-Barker" once again surfaced when she ordered Robert to go to the local exterminator supply store and purchase two-gallons of their most powerful, pure, weed-killer that money could buy! She also bought a commercial pump sprayer.

When Robert returned with the weed-killer, mama ordered him to fill the pump sprayer with the raw chemical. It didn't matter to mama that the instructions read to mix *one-part* weed killer to *ten-parts* water.

Mama then ordered Robert to go over in her neighbor's yard and to soak a strip no less than ten-feet wide, from the front of his yard to the end at the back yard. To soak everything that adjoins mama's lawn to the neighbors!

The neighbor was at work when Robert emptied the sprayer on the man's lawn as mama had ordered. She ordered Robert to put the other gallon of weed killer in the sprayer and soak it again!

Needless to say, within a couple of days, there was nothing living or left standing in the neighbor's yard. No grass, no weeds, no bugs and no germ could have survived this treatment. Not even the dirt itself could ever serve any useful purpose again!

There was a long black ten-foot strip that ran from the neighbor's front property line to his back property line, that Robert and myself referred to as; "death-valley."

Needless to say, the neighbor who looks like a professional wrestler from the WWF, came walking up to mama's front screen door, and asked her if she knew what had happened to his lawn. Mama, who is never short for words, proceeded to shout at him, that he had plenty of warning to control his dollar-weed, and did nothing about it.

Her exact words were: "If you are too damned sorry to care for your lawn, and want to lay around on your fat ass drinking beer all day and night, then I'll take care of your problem myself!"

"If that ten-foot strip doesn't stop your dollar-weed from crawling onto my lawn, then I'll spray your entire yard next time!"

He threatened to file a law-suit against mama, and walked away!

Robert was shaking in his shoes while hiding behind mama's back.

Robert thanked God that the man didn't kick his ass before walking away!

No grass or dollar-weed ever came back to the neighbor's lawn, and so far, no legal action has ever been taken concerning this incident.

Mama was never worried about it anyway.

MAMA KNOWS BASEBALL

Once before I retired, I was on a business trip to Jacksonville and took the opportunity to visit with mama and Robert. I always stayed overnight at mama' house when I was in the area.

We had just finished with our dinner when the three of us settled down in the living room to relax and watch television.

Robert was in control of the remote, and was flicking through the channels when he settled on an Atlanta Braves baseball game. As the game progressed, mama suddenly said; "that just ain't right or fair!"

Robert replied; "what ain't right or fair?"

Mama said; "that pitcher!, He's throwing the ball to that man squatting down behind the plate, and he's suppose to be throwing the ball at the batter!"

Robert said; "the pitcher is suppose to throw the ball to the man squatting down, he's the catcher!"

Mama said; "I know better, the pitcher is suppose to throw the ball at the batter!"

Robert said; "there ain't no batter in his right mind who would stand there and let a pitcher throw ninety-mile per hour baseballs at him!"

Mama said; "well how is the batter suppose to hit the ball, if the pitcher is throwing the ball at the man squatting down?"

Mama then said; "I know baseball, cause when I was a young lady in high school, I played on a team!"... "The pitcher is suppose to throw the ball at the batter!"

Robert said; "If the pitcher throws the ball at the batter, how is the batter suppose to hit the damn thing?"

"The batter would either be seriously injured or killed!"

Mama said; "well, I know better, and I don't understand why that other man in the black suit is standing there shouting, shaking his arms and interfering with the game!"... "Somebody ought to make him get off the field too!"

Robert said; "that man in the black suit is the umpire, he calls the strikes and balls!"

Mama said; "well he's disrupting the game as far as I'm concerned!"

Mama was ninety-three years of age, so Robert knew better than to continue an argument that he couldn't possibly win. He just shut up!

I was just sitting there thanking God that Robert had the strength to handle mama, and humor her! This is normal daily conversation between mama and Robert.

Since mama supports and gives Robert a roof over his head, this is a good arrangement for both of them. For his keep, Robert lives with and looks after mama in her senior years.

If Robert was unable, or refused to care for mama in her old age, that job would fall in my lap!

Hang in there Robert!... I have personally asked God to bless you.

MY BEST ALL TIME FRIEND

I cannot close out this book without acknowledging my very best all time friend, Frank Tyler. We met as youngsters playing street ball and instantly bonded. Fifty eight years later, we are as close as any two brothers.

I have enough memories to write an entire novel on the adventures that we experienced together over the years. We were both dirt poor and lived less than five blocks from each other in Jacksonville.

Frank's mother passed away before he and I met, and he was pretty much left to fend for himself.

I remember that Frank's father was a heavy drinker. He wasn't a cruel or non-caring person, but he didn't have the means or savvy to raise a child alone.

They lived in an apartment above a small mattress factory where Frank's father worked. Their living conditions were less than adequate, but served it's purpose for the two of them.

Frank's father would always hit the road with a lady friend as soon as he got off work in the afternoon, and was away most weekends.

This left Frank and I the freedom to use the apartment to do what ever we found to be fun. The place was so old and dilapidated, that we would hang targets on the bedroom walls and shoot at them for hours with a 22-rifle! Forty or fifty bullet holes in the walls made little or no difference, and were seldom noticed by his father!

On occasion, Frank's father would bring a woman home to have a little romp in the hay. They would both be so drunk, that Frank and I were mostly ignored. As curious kids, we would sometimes hide, watch and laugh at the live porno show.

Frank and I were always hungry, so we would cook a meal quite often in the old kitchen on the kerosene stove. Don't ask me why, but we usually cooked the same thing; pork chops, pork-n-beans, sliced avocado with mayonnaise, bread & butter.

As we grew older, we graduated from our bicycles and managed to buy our first (really used) motor scooters. Mine was a traditional style Cushman Motor Scooter, while Frank's was a more custom style Cushman Eagle.

We virtually lived on those things and through trial and error, discovered how to make our own repairs and do some things to make them go faster.

On weekends when nobody was there, Frank would open the mattress work shop area and we would go in and use their sewing machines and upholstery materials to make seat covers and fancy trim for our scooters.

If you can imagine the old stories of Huckleberry Finn and his buddies; this was us. We would build a raft out of scrap wood and float up and down the St. Johns River, exploring what ever we could find. If we were not in school, we were inseparable.

As time passed, the teen years came along and we upgraded our motor scooters to motorcycles. Speed was our thing and even today, we reminisce and wonder how we weren't killed. We were arrested a few times and charged with speeding and reckless driving.

I remember once, when we were arrested and put in jail. Frank's father bailed him out that same day, while I spent an additional twelve-days for contempt of court. Nothing criminal, just traffic violations!

Then another time, I was riding double, behind Frank on his motorcycle on Jacksonville Beach. The police stopped us again for speeding.

They put us both in the police car and took us to jail. Frank was put in a cell, but since I was only his passenger, they told me I could go.

Frank's motorcycle was a very fast chopper and I could see it parked in the police department's impound lot.

Standing on the sidewalk next to the police station, I was able to talk to Frank through his cell window.

I knew that he had already called his father to come and bail him out, so I shouted to Frank that I was going to take his motorcycle and ride it home. He said it was okay, that he would get a ride home with his father.

The gate to the police impound lot was open, and there wasn't anyone on duty where the motorcycle was parked. I rolled the motorcycle off it's stand and pushed it out to the street before firing it up.

I knew that once the police discovered the motorcycle was missing, they would come after me with everyone they had!

I kick-started the cycle and took off like a bat out of hell! Frank later told me that about fifteen minutes after I rode off, the police discovered the motorcycle was missing, and knew that I had taken it!

Frank said that the police dispatcher called all of their units to intercept me, to include the Florida Highway Patrol and the Jacksonville Sheriff's Department Dispatchers.

Frank said he could hear me way off in the distance winding out the gears and speed shifting. He knew I was long gone, and even had the balls to tell the dispatcher: "you'll never catch him!"

They didn't catch me, and since I wasn't part of the original arrest, they didn't even know my name. Frank lied and told the police that he had only met me that day, and he didn't know my name either!

Thank God I wasn't caught, because I would have been charged with Felony Grand-Theft!

A few months later, Frank and I were fortunate enough to convince the best looking twin-sisters in Jacksonville to double-date with us on our motorcycles. These twins were awesome, had bodies right out of Penthouse Magazine and were two hot commodities!

When we picked them up, they both had on white short-shorts. Just the sight of them would take a man's breath away!

I do remember it had just started to rain lightly, but we took off with them anyway. We were rounding a sharp curve on Post Street, when Frank's motorcycle suddenly slipped out from under him and they went down. Both he and the beauty riding with him, hit the pavement and started to slide. Needless to say, they both got skinned-up a little and were lying in the middle of the street.

Frank jumped up and quickly picked up his motorcycle and put in on it's kick-stand. By then, the twin riding with him had gotten to her feet.

I never will forget that girl, mad as hell, yelling at Frank as to why he picked up his motorcycle first, leaving her lying in the street.

Frank replied: "because there was no battery-acid running out of you!"

He went on to explain to her that a motorcycle laying on it's side, would cause battery-acid to run out and permanently damage any chrome or paint that it came in contact with.

Both the twins were furious and demanded that we take them home. I still grieve over the fact that we lost a great opportunity to possibly make out with two of Jacksonville's finest!

Time heals everything and although we didn't get the booty that day, we still laugh about the battery-acid incident!

I remember once that Frank and I rode our motorcycles out to the State Fair that was in town. He had enough change for us to go inside and watch the freak show.

One performer took a long sharp ice-pick and ran it all the way up his nose, into his face!

We were really impressed with this stunt, so I told Frank lets wait till all the people leave the tent, and we'll ask the performer how he did that. Once the tent was empty, we walked over to the performer and I said: "mister, do you really shove that ice-pick up your nose?

He looked at us and screamed: "hell no, I shove it up my ass!" He then not so politely told us to get the hell out of his tent!

We laugh about that now, but at the time, he scared the shit out of us!

Frank was a true friend that I could always depend on. He was always there for me, as I was for him.

We both served honorably in the military. Frank in the Marines and myself in the Air Force.

To this day, we still remain just as close and spend some quality time fishing and talking about old times. My wife and I have an open invitation to visit with Frank and his wife Brenda at their river front home.

I don't know who will outlive who, but you can bet your bottom-dollar that when one of us has gone, there will be a great void left in the survivors life!

Thank you Frank for remaining my friend for all these years. You had a massive impact and made a positive contribution to my life.

MAMA WAS OVERLY PROTECTIVE

As I mentioned earlier, mama was extremely overly protective where her children were concerned. The discipline she dished out was many times brutal and at other times, made so sense what-so-ever.

A good example; "you can't go swimming till you learn how to swim!" "You will drown!" How the hell were we going to learn how to swim, if we were never allowed to get near the water?

As a youngster, there were many times, that I would sneak away with my buddy Frank Tyler and go swimming or rafting. Instead of swimming at a supervised park, pool or lake, we ended up swimming or rafting in the St. Johns River, rated as one of most treacherous rivers in the U.S. This being far more dangerous than swimming at a public location where there were life-guards!

I remember I was fifteen years old, and was already (unbeknown to mama) ranked among some of the top motorcycle racers in the State of Florida. My good friend Milton Ricks who owned the BSA Motorcycle Shop in Jacksonville was my racing sponsor and had scheduled me to race at the Waycross, Georgia Speedway.

Instead of lying or sneaking away like in the past, I confided in mama and explained that Mr. Ricks would pick me up in his car, with the motorcycle and trailer attached. That we would take a slow, safe ride to Georgia, where I would race under safe, controlled conditions. Boy was that a mistake!

Mama started yelling ; "you ain't going, you ain't going nowhere to race!" "You'll crash or fall and be crippled or killed!" "Hell no, you ain't going!"

To calm mama and keep her from having a stroke, I agreed not to go, and called Milton Ricks to so advise. I did tell him that if I could get away, I would show up in Waycross. Milton left for Georgia alone!

Now mama thought she was protecting me from injury or death by refusing to allow me to travel and race that day. She knew the race was scheduled to begin at 1:00 P.M. and decided to keep me in her sight until she was comfortable that it was too late for me to make it to the race.

She had no idea just what massive danger she had put me in.

Now picture this: At 11:45 A.M, she was confident that it was safe to allow me to leave the house. She said: "I know you're mad at me, but I just couldn't allow you to race and get hurt!" With this statement, she said it was okay for me to leave the house if I wanted.

If she only knew, this would have been where her worst nightmare was to begin! I knew that I had one-hour and fifteen minutes to travel from Jacksonville, Florida to Waycross, Georgia, and still make it in time for the first qualifying race.

I gently rode away from mama's house at a nice slow pace, until I reached the first intersection. Heading straight for Interstate 95, I opened the throttle full-bore and kept it open for the next eighty-five miles. Traveling at speeds well over one-hundred miles per hour, for the next sixty-minutes, I made it to the speedway just moments before the first qualifying race.

How I made it to Waycross in one piece, without being killed or arrested, could only be explained, that my Guardian Angel was riding with me!

I did race and did come home with the first-place trophy. Milton Ricks displayed the trophy in his motorcycle shop, because I couldn't take it home under the circumstances.

Later that evening, mama asked what I had done all day, and I told her that I spent the afternoon with my girlfriend.

If mama only knew what danger she had put me in, while thinking she was protecting me from harm!

EPILOGUE
THE SAVAGE CLAN

FATE OF BILLY AND SARAH'S CHILDREN

Roger Savage:
By the Grace of God, Roger survived Billy's wrath until he was seventeen, when he ran away from home, scarred for life, both mentally and physically. He only returned home long enough to attend his siblings funerals. The day after each funeral, Roger left again. He is believed to be living someplace in Kentucky.

Mary Lynn Savage:
Mary Lynn was Billy and Sarah's first daughter, who suffered much greater hardships than her younger sister Grace. Like her brothers and sister, all she ever knew was pure-hell on earth living with Billy's wrath. Mary Lynn not only suffered physical and mental abuses, she also suffered sexual abuses.

Sarah suspected that Billy was sexually abusing Mary Lynn, but was either too afraid to confront Billy, or was just ignorant enough to close her mind to what was going on!

I won't try to second guess Sarah's failure to protect her daughter, because I know first hand the savage brutality that she also endured.

A person can only stand torture for so long, and the mind will break. Sarah endured continuous torture from Billy for more than thirty-years.

Mary Lynn was a young teen when Billy decided that she needed to know the touch of a man. Since none of the children were allowed out in the real world and none had ever had a boyfriend or girlfriend, Billy thought it was now his responsibility to teach Mary Lynn about the "birds and the bees!"

Billy's teaching wasn't just verbal, it was physical as well!

After the children were put to bed, Billy and Sarah would go to bed.

Billy would lay there for about thirty-minutes and then quietly slip out of bed and disappear down the dark hallway of the house.

Sarah died a thousand deaths when Billy did this, because she knew in her heart that Billy was in Mary Lynn's bedroom. Sarah tried to convince herself that it wasn't really happening, that it was just a figment of her imagination... but she knew better!

Mary Lynn took the abuses from Billy for as long as she could, before she ran away from home.

Mary Lynn ended up in New Orleans, Louisiana where she met a chauvinist pig son-of-a-bitch, who offered her a place to live and then took total advantage of her introverted ignorance.

Mary Lynn immediately became pregnant and gave birth to a daughter before she was abandoned by the pig she was living with.

She was living in a run down motel that was converted into less than adequate efficiency apartments.

With no means to survive financially, and even less desire to live, Mary Lynn called her younger brother Jake, who hitch-hiked to New Orleans to be with his sister.

When Jake arrived at the motel about three o'clock in the afternoon, he found Mary Lynn and her baby daughter living in poverty.

At six o'clock, Mary Lynn told Jake that she needed to go

grocery shopping, and asked Jake to watch her baby till she got back.

She picked up her daughter and spent several minutes, as Jake remembered, just hugging and kissing her goodbye!

Mary Lynn then hugged Jake and thanked him for coming to help her, before she drove away in an old junker car.

Jake and the baby fell asleep waiting for Mary Lynn to return, but she never did!

Early the next morning, two police officers were banging on the motel door to awaken Jake. The officers asked Jake to identify himself, which he did, before he was told that his sister Mary Lynn had committed suicide!

Jake had no choice but to take the baby and return home to Billy's house of horrors! Sarah took the baby in and raised the child as her own.

Police investigation reports and witness's statements later gave the following account of Mary Lynn's suicide:

Two barge welders were working at the Mississippi river-front levee, when they spotted Mary Lynn drive into the large gravel parking area of the boat-yard.

Her car was about one-hundred yards away, facing the levee, with the motor running and the headlights on.

Now for the reader that doesn't know what a Louisiana Levee is, let me explain:

In New Orleans as with much of Louisiana, the Mississippi River is a most important part of the economy. The river is wide and runs swiftly to support the massive shipping and barge industry.

Because of flooding problems, large man-made levees are built on both sides of the Mississippi to protect from flooding.

A levee is a very large mound that reaches elevated levels of twenty to forty feet or taller, depending on the flood areas past history.

The best way I know to describe a levee would be to imagine the motorcycle ramp that Evel Kenevel built in his attempt to jump the Grand-Canyon.

When the two welders witnessed Mary Lynn's car parked facing the levee (ramp), they could see her sitting behind the wheel staring straight ahead, like in a trance. The car sat there for about five minutes, when the engine started to race.

The wheels started spinning in the gravel, as the car lunged forward running wide open toward the levee ramp.

By the time the car reached the levee, she was at full throttle.

Mary's car hit the ramp leaping over the top and sailing approximately forty-feet out into the Mississippi, coming nose down into the river.

The two welders watched in shock, as the car sank below the muddy, dark surface, leaving only bubbles. Mary Lynn Savage was dead!

Mary Lynn has no grave marker.

Roger Savage returned home to attend Mary Lynn's funeral and then left the following day.

Tommy Savage:
Tommy survived until he was twenty-two. He too was scarred for life like the other children in his family, a complete introvert with no hope for his future.

Tommy found some way to get his hands on a pistol. He walked down the street from his home and deliberately caused a disturbance, demanding that someone call the police. Tommy just stood there on the sidewalk a few blocks from where he lived, holding the pistol at his side.

Within minutes, five police cruisers were on the scene. The officers demanded that Tommy drop the gun, but Tommy just stood there for almost ten-minutes staring at the police and ignoring their demands.

He then smiled at the police officers, raised his pistol and pointed it directly at them.

Fourteen rounds ripped through the flesh of Tommy's body as he fell to the pavement.

Tommy never fired a shot! He had no criminal record or previous trouble with the law.

Roger returned for Tommy's funeral and left the following day.

Tommy has no grave marker! He was buried as he was forced to live, with no dignity.

Grace Savage:
Grace Savage grieving over the suicides of Mary Lynn and Tommy, came to the conclusion that they were both better off dead and she wanted to be with them.

Within ten-months of Tommy's death, Grace Savage also committed suicide with a massive over-dose of medications.

Grace has no grave marker.

Roger Savage again returned to attend the funeral of his sister Grace, and left the following day.

Jake Savage:
Jake ran away from home and never returned. He is believed to be living somewhere in Texas.

Leonard Savage:
Leonard ran away from home and never returned.

For years, he was working as a security guard some where in Miami, Florida. Leonard had no contact with his parents after leaving home, until someone years later called his mother, to tell her that Leonard was dying of Lou Gehrig's disease. Leonard lived long enough for his mother and myself to visit with him in a nursing home.

Leonard was paralyzed from the neck down when we found him. Able to speak only short sentences, Leonard told both his mother and myself that he loved us before he died!

Leonard was buried without a stone or marker in a pauper's graveyard!

Roger Savage returned for Leonard's funeral and left the following day.

God bless you Leonard, and I will see you again in Heaven.

Michael Savage:

Michael ran away from home and chose a military career. He is married and has two children. Michael spent most of his career in Germany where he retired.

Michael calls his mother on occasion.

FATE OF BILLY AND SARAH SAVAGE

Sarah finally ordered Billy out of her house after thirty-five years of marriage, but didn't finalize their divorce for another five-years.

She is seventy three years of age at the time of this writing. She lives in a public-housing unit in Sanford, Florida, on partial welfare, with one of her granddaughters, (the daughter of Mary Lynn who committed suicide in New Orleans). Sarah currently works in a high-school cafeteria.

Billy moved into a run down dilapidated mobile-home, in a senior park near Sanford, where he spent his days and nights sucking on beer and whiskey bottles.

He remained there in a drunken stupor for the next six years, until he died of cancer.

When Billy was admitted to the hospital just days before his death, I was led by the Holy Spirit to go to him, regardless of how brutally he had treated me as a child.

When I entered his hospital room, he was semi-conscious. I noticed his eye-glasses held together by tape and wire, lying on the end table. I picked them up and placed them on Billy's face, waking him up.

He just stared at me when I asked him if he knew who I was.

Staring at me for a few more seconds, Billy said; "no sir, I don't believe I do!"

I said to Billy; "I'm your baby brother, Johnny!"

With that, Billy broke down and started to cry, because he hadn't seen me in many years.

Knowing that Billy was slipping closer to death, I said to him; "Billy, I must ask you a serious question, and I want you to be truthful with me!"

I then said; "Billy are you saved, have you accepted Jesus Christ as your Lord and personal saviour?"

Billy looked me straight in the eyes and said; "Johnny, I know that I haven't lived a good life and I know that I've done some horrible things!"

He then said; "the answer to your question is yes, I have asked Jesus to come into my heart and to forgive me of my sins!"

Billy then asked me; "are you saved Johnny?" ... I replied; "yes I am!"

That was pretty much the last conversation I had with Billy, because he slipped deeper into a coma and died within days.

I told mama about my conversation with Billy and how I had humored him one last time before he died, by expressing a brotherly love toward him as best I could. Mama was really happy to know that Billy was saved. Mama and Robert saw him one last time.

Mama paid the expenses for Billy's funeral. All his surviving children were there out of respect for their mother. They left the next day and have never had conversation again with Sarah, with exception of Michael, who is in the military, stationed in Germany.

May God have mercy on every member of the Savage clan and to all our descendants, dead or alive!

HAROLD'S OLD RICH WITCH VISITS MAMA

Now what do you make of this? ... After more than ten-years of silence, Harold's rich widow decides to call mama on July 19, 2000 and request permission to visit her, along with her two daughters, their husbands and children.

Why, after all these years of silence? Both Harold and Agnes had ignored mama, refused to visit, call, or even acknowledge her existence, not even in Harold's eulogies. Why did Agnes and her family choose to suddenly show up on mama's doorstep?

Well, whatever the reason, mama said "yes", and welcomed them with open arms, when they arrived on Sunday, July 23, 2000, with two buckets of Kentucky Fried Chicken!

Before their arrival, mama begged Robert to stay and greet them, when she learned that he had made arrangements to get the hell out of the house, before they arrived.

Both Robert and I refused to meet or greet the enemy, even though mama had decided to forgive and forget!

There was no way in hell that I could have stood to look into Agnes's evil face after what she and Harold had done to mama and this family over the years.

In respect to mama, Robert did stay at the house, but he remained on the front porch all day smoking his cigarettes. He refused to go inside to listen to the slobbering excuses as to why they had avoided mama for the past ten-years. For the next six hours, Robert could hear them sucking up to mama. All that bullshit was enough to make him want to puke.

After the visit, mama called me on the phone to assure me that my name was never mentioned during the visit. I thanked mama for that honor!

Three days after the visit, Robert called to ask me the following: "why do you suppose Agnes decided to call mama and request permission to visit, after a ten-year absence?"

I replied to Robert with the following: "do you remember when grandma died? Within twenty-four hours, Harold stripped her house of every valuable antique and collectable, and took it for himself."

"Do you remember when Harold and Agnes declared our parents to be dead, disowned all of the family, and stayed away for thirteen-years?"

"Do you remember when our father died, and Harold suddenly appeared on mama's door step, offering to search the house and attics, looking for Sylvester's hidden cash?"

"Do you remember that Harold told mama that he didn't find anything, when all of the family knew damned well that Sylvester had a small fortune in cash, hidden somewhere in the house or attics?"

"Do you remember that before Harold left the house, he talked mama into signing over her valuable thirteen-acre track of land in Oneida, Tennessee?" With the property in his name, he drove away, never to return again, right up to his death, ten-years later.

"Do you know that it takes two or more witnesses to sign and verify a document to be legal, if you don't have a notary as a witness?"

"Don't you wonder why Agnes brought her two daughters and their husbands for an unexpected visit after a ten-year absence?"

"Do you wonder if it has anything to do with mama being ninety-two years of age, and near death?"

"Do you wonder if Agnes and her two daughters may have talked mama into signing a blank legal-document known as a "Will", before they gave her a hug and departed after the visit?"

"Do you believe Agnes is low enough to use her two daughters and their husbands to witness a will, that mama didn't understand, or know it's content... .with blanks that could be filled-in later?"

I then told Robert, if my suspicions are correct, you won't hear another word from Agnes or her daughters, until mama's death.

At that point in time, Agnes will produce a new will, signed by mama and witnessed by her daughters and their husbands.

This new legal-document will show Agnes as the executor to mama's estate, with everything legally left to her and her daughters.

I told Robert again, if my suspicions are correct, he will be written out of mama's will, and his ass will be sleeping in a cardboard-box under some bridge, when mama passes on!

This is just a suspicion on my part, but knowing Harold and Agnes as I do, I suspect that Agnes has cut mama's throat one last time before she dies!

As for Robert and me, we aren't virgins. We've been screwed so many times, that one more ass-reaming won't make a difference.

Who really gives a shit anymore?

FATE OF BRUCE SAVAGE, SON OF JOHNNY

In 2001, my son Bruce was 41 years of age when he closed his business (Sports Bar) at a Florida resort beach area. It was about 1:30 A.M. when he called for a taxi, to take him to meet some friends at a local beach-front cocktail lounge.

While attempting to exit the taxi, two men jumped my son and beat him to death. Leaving my son bleeding and lying on the sidewalk, they fled the scene in the same taxi, by threatening the driver. Before making their exit from the taxi, they warned the driver if he talked, he would get some of the same!

It has been assumed that the two men thought my son had the days business deposit on him after closing. They did take his gold necklace and a bracelet that his children had given him for Christmas.

The two men killed my son for nothing, because the day's business deposit was secure back in the club's safe.

The taxi driver and two witnesses provided the police investigator with very accurate composite drawings of the two suspects.

Valuable leads and identifications of one of the suspects fell upon deaf ears and is now in the dead case files, buried somewhere in the bottom of a dusty cabinet.

I might add, that the taxi driver became so afraid, that he refused to talk further to the police, hired an attorney and moved to south Georgia. Within six months, the taxi driver in question, was found dead. Autopsy found that he had been poisoned!

As of the date of this writing, police investigators still haven't solved either case!

The loss of my only son has been devastating to all the family. Bruce left behind a wife and six children. Many underwent counseling.

FATE OF SYLVIA, ROBERT AND JOHNNY SAVAGE

Sylvia Savage:
Sylvia Savage is ninety-seven years of age at this writing. She still lives in the same home she purchased when she and the children tried to escape from Sylvester.

For her age, she is doing all right, living on her Social Security and pension from the Southern Bell Telephone Company. She never had much when she was living with Sylvester, so she doesn't expect much even today.

Sylvia is growing weaker day by day, but living comfortably. She still has a reasonably sharp mind, but her legs just don't want to carry her anymore.

She loves the Lord Jesus with all her heart and enjoys her remaining years, close to her sons, Robert & Johnny.

Robert Savage:
Robert Savage a die-hard bachelor is sixty-nine years of age at this writing and lives with mama in Jacksonville, Florida.

Robert was a great help to mama. Until he became ill himself. He maintained her lawn and shrubs, took her to and from her doctor appointments, grocery shopping, and in general ran her errands.

In exchange, he continues to live free of costs with mama, like he has for the past twenty-eight years.

Robert is too sick to leave the house, so he still remains unemployed. He draws Social Security and stays in his bedroom sleeping most of the day and night.

Due to his health, he hasn't left the house in many years.

Robert still has a serious case of OCD, but somewhat content with his lifestyle.

I'm happy that he is there with mama every day and night, so they can at least watch over each other!

Sick or not, Robert is the only thing keeping mama out of a nursing home.

Her sight is extremely bad, she can barely walk, and spends most of her days in a hospital bed.

Johnny Savage:
My life long career choice was law-enforcement, criminal-justice and corporate loss-prevention. I retired on December 1, 2003.

I will devote the remainder of my healthy years watching over mama and Robert, for as long as they live.

If my health holds out, I will continue teaching the martial arts, which has been a committed part of my life for the past fifty-years. I will need this to supplement my retirement income.

In storage, I have all the equipment necessary, to open a small training facility, where I will teach three or four nights a week.

I will travel some weekends conducting seminars and clinics throughout the United States. I will also hold one major summer training camp each year.

Thank you God for allowing the three of us to survive!

DOMESTIC VIOLENCE

Domestic violence is not a simple broken nose or black eye. Domestic violence is defined as power and control of one family member over another.

Domestic violence is controlling behavior, it is constant criticism, it is belittling remarks that slowly eat away at a person's very being.

Emotional abuse is just as detrimental as physical abuse. Where broken bones heal, verbal abuse scars your very soul and remains for life.

∞

FLOWERS

I got flowers today. It wasn't my birthday or any other special day. We had our first argument last night, and he said a lot of cruel things that really hurt me.

I know he is sorry and didn't mean the things he said, because he sent me flowers today.

It wasn't our anniversary or any other special day. Last night, he threw me into a wall and started to choke me. It seemed like a nightmare. I couldn't believe it was real.

I woke up this morning sore and bruised all over. I know he must be sorry, because he sent me flowers today.

I got flowers today, and it wasn't Mothers Day or any other special day.

Last night, he beat me up again, and it was much worse than all the other times.

If I leave him, what will I do? How will I take care of my kids? What about money?

I'm afraid of him and scared to leave. But I know he must be sorry because he sent me flowers today.

Today was a very special day. It was the day of my funeral.

Last night, he finally killed me. He beat me to death.

If I had only gathered strength to leave him, I would not have gotten flowers today.

(Unknown Author /
A printing from Citrus County Abuse Shelter Association)

FINAL CHAPTER

On *October 17, 2005,* Sylvia "Ma-Barker" Savage, at the age of *ninety seven*, went on to meet her maker and be united with her family again. May she live in peace for eternity.

Robert now alone, was relocated from Jacksonville to Central Florida by his brother Johnny, where they reside just blocks from each other.

On _____, Robert D. Savage, at the age of _____, did as usual and followed after mama. I am sure that he is still living in mama's heavenly mansion, and will remain there for eternity.

On _____, Johnny Savage, at the age of _____, followed after mama and Robert. He too will live there for eternity, and if God has allowed, he will still remain close by, to watch over mama and Robert!

"No, we are not dead yet. We live on in heaven!"

NOTES

ISBN 1412089255